F.M.

UNIVERSITY COLLEGE LIBRARY

Two week
loan

Please return on or before the last
date stamped below.
Charges are made for late return.

2 3 APR 1998		
	1 4 JUN 2002	
29 MAY 1998	1 7 JUL 2002	
2 8 SEP 1998		
	9 AUG 2002	
- 1 JUN 1999		
2 8 MAY 1999		
2 7 MAR 2000		
- 3 MAY 2000		
- 4 OCT 2000		

THE FINANCING OF SMALL BUSINESS

Also by the Author
(with J. R. Parkinson)
"Business Economics." Blackwell: 1963
Second edition 1969

AUSTRALIA
The Law Book Company Ltd.
Sydney : Melbourne : Brisbane

CANADA AND U.S.A.
The Carswell Company Ltd.
Agincourt, Ontario

INDIA
N. M. Tripathi Private Ltd.
Bombay

ISRAEL
Steimatzky's Agency Ltd.
Jerusalem : Tel Aviv : Haifa

MALAYSIA: SINGAPORE: BRUNEI
Malayan Law Journal (Pte) Ltd.
Singapore

NEW ZEALAND
Sweet & Maxwell (N.Z.) Ltd.
Wellington

PAKISTAN
Pakistan Law House
Karachi

THE FINANCING
OF
SMALL BUSINESS

BY

JAMES BATES

Professor of Business Economics, Queen's University, Belfast

SECOND EDITION

LONDON
SWEET & MAXWELL
1971

First edition 1964
Second edition 1971
Published by
Sweet & Maxwell Ltd. of
11 New Fetter Lane, London
and filmset in Photon Times 11 on 12 pt. by
Richard Clay (The Chaucer Press) Ltd., Bungay, Suffolk
and printed in Great Britain by
Fletcher & Son, Ltd., Norwich, Norfolk

SBN 421 13810 6

PREFACE TO THE FIRST EDITION

THE main purpose of this book is to examine the financial problems of the small business from two points of view: that of the economist and that of the owner or financial adviser of the small firm; and it attempts to do this in two ways. The first of these consists of a systematic outline of the main sources of funds available to small firms, and an account of the major problems and difficulties associated with them. At the same time the book includes the results of an inquiry into the financial affairs of small and medium-sized manufacturing firms carried out by the Oxford University Institute of Statistics during 1956: the purpose and background data of the Small Business Survey and the methods of analysis of the data are outlined in Appendix A, the relevant details appear in appropriate chapters. The analysis of the results of the Survey provides some factual information on which to base a discussion of these important practical problems, in a field which has been singularly ill-documented.

The first two chapters consist of an examination in general terms of the problems of small firms and the principles of finance. The next six chapters set out each of the main sources of funds and analyse them in some detail, both from the point of view of the firm and from the point of view of the economist. The small firm faces particular difficulties in each field in which it attempts to raise funds: I have discussed these and shown reasons for them, and attempted to show ways in which some of the difficulties may be overcome. Some of the problems may be solved by the firms themselves or by their economic advisers; some could be overcome by changes in the practices of financial institutions; others are more far-reaching and are the subject of economic policy. In the final chapter I have attempted to draw together the main threads and to point the economic lessons of the study and to look at some further implications.

In order not to interrupt the text too much I have put a great deal of the statistical material into tables in the Appendices, and have made reference where necessary in the appropriate chapters, confining statistical material in the text to data necessary to illustrate particular points. Appendix A contains the background data from the

Small Business Survey; Appendix B contains a few tables with information on the place of small firms in the economy; Appendix C consists of a detailed breakdown of balance-sheet information in the form of simple frequency distributions of each main item.

The analysis of the data from the Survey is not elaborate or statistical, and is more in the nature of a description of the salient features. I have not subjected the data to statistical testing, and on the occasions when I have referred to relationships between two variables I should like to make it clear that I am suggesting rather than proving hypotheses from the data. The full-scale statistical or economic analysis of the data I have regarded as a separate task: some of this is now in progress. The examination of the data presented here fulfils my present purpose of outlining the main problems and attaching some orders of magnitude to the entities involved.

My interest in these problems is determined largely by my qualifications to discuss them: it is that of the practical economist and not that of the accountant. I have therefore used the methods and terminology of the economist, and have tried not to exceed this function. This does mean that there may be some confusion over terminology, and in particular over the use of the word "firm." Accountants give this word a very limited meaning: that of a number of people acting together in the form of a partnership. I have used the word in the economist's sense to mean any business enterprise, regardless of its legal form, and this is the meaning which this word has whenever it appears in this book. When I have wished to distinguish between legal forms I have referred to them by their proper names: sole owners or partnerships I have referred to either by those names or together as "unincorporated businesses"; companies I have distinguished according to whether they are public or private, quoted or unquoted, exempt or non-exempt, as the occasion has demanded.

Acknowledgments

The Small Business Survey was financed by a grant made under the Conditional Aid Scheme for the use of counterpart funds derived from United States Economic Aid; and was planned and executed by a team consisting of H. F. Lydall, M. J. Stewart and myself. A pilot study had previously been carried out by the late F. A. Burchardt, Colin Bruce and E. B. Gibb, who also took part in the planning of the main Survey. Fieldwork was carried out by the Social Survey department of the Central Office of Information; some preliminary tabulations were carried out by the Tabulating Research Centre in London; both of these operations were directed by J. E. Fothergill, formerly of the Social Survey and now of British Market Research Bureau. At the same time research was being conducted at the National Institute of Economic and Social Research into the finance of quoted public companies, under the direction of Brian Tew and R. F. Henderson; all concerned with this project gave invaluable help and consultation in the planning and analysis stages of the Small Business Survey.

The processing of data, much of the preliminary analysis, and the typing of a draft report on the financial aspects of the Survey were all done at the Institute of Statistics, and I should like to acknowledge my debt to the Director (the late F. A. Burchardt) and Acting Director (K. G. J. C. Knowles) for making the facilities available and to thank all of the people who helped with the vast amount of detailed work. In 1959 I took up an appointment in the Department of Social and Economic Research in the University of Glasgow where, thanks to the understanding and generosity of the Head of the Department, Professor A. K. Cairncross, who gave me the time and the facilities, I was able to complete the analysis of the data and write a first draft of the present book.

The present version owes a great deal to the advice and criticism of my colleagues. In addition to those already mentioned, without whose co-operation the project would probably never have got off the ground, I also thank those who read and criticised an earlier draft of this book—in particular A. K. Cairncross, P. E. Hart, R. F. Henderson, N. Momtchiloff and D. J. Robertson—and all of my colleagues, past and present, who have been ready to help with advice and criticism. I have lived with the problems of business finance for so many years and have discussed them with so many people that it would be difficult to sort out which were my own ideas and which came from other people.

Two other acknowledgments I must make separately. First is to the man without whom this work would probably never have been done—the late Frank Burchardt, who was Director of the Institute of Statistics during the period when this Survey was carried out. In addition to the intellectual stimulus which he imparted to all who came in contact with him, his advice and encouragement were a never-failing source of help. And finally I must make much more than the conventional acknowledgment to my wife who throughout has helped me with calculations, the preparation of tables and the typing of the manuscript, and who has been a patient and never-failing source of encouragement.

To all of these thanks I must of course add a reminder that responsibility for the many faults which remain is mine alone.

University of Bristol,   JAMES BATES
May 1963.

I am grateful to the Editors of *The Bankers' Magazine* and *The Banker* for permission to use material previously published in those journals.

PREFACE TO THE SECOND EDITION

THIS edition is more like a new book than a revision. In the early stages of rewriting it became clear that it would not be worth while merely to make small amendments. The data from the Small Business Survey could not be brought up to date, and it was not necessary to reproduce the survey report in its entirety; accordingly whilst reference is frequently made to the survey, to the first edition and to subsequent publications based on the survey, the details are not included. It also seemed desirable to make the second edition more of a guide for the owner and manager of a small business, and in pursuit of this aim a number of new sections have been included on financial planning and other practical matters; the sections on sources of funds have also been substantially rewritten. There are also notes, where relevant, on the consequences of recent company legislation, notably the Finance Act 1965 and the Companies Act 1967, which both brought changes in the financial scene.

Thus this is now a book of guidelines for the financing of small business, based on research and my own experience. The first and last chapters look at broader issues: the first discusses the importance of small businesses in the economy, and looks at some of their problems; the last examines ways in which some of the problems might be tackled, and looks at possible improvements.

I have stuck to the terminology of the first edition, and in particular have used the word "firm" to mean any business enterprise; this usage is that of the economist and has been for at least two centuries; it is also that of the Radcliffe Committee and the Bolton Committee. Although this book deals with problems which are also the concern of the accounting and legal professions I am not a member of those professions, and my comments must be seen as those of the business economist and the business adviser.

A number of acknowledgments and thanks must be added to those of the first edition. For discussions with members of the Bolton Committee (both as private individuals and as members) I am grateful: I learnt a lot, clarified many ideas, and was forced to think again about many of them; but they are in no way to blame for what appears here, which in no sense previews their report. My colleagues

Mr. P. Quinn and Mr. D. Rea have been an invaluable source of help and, since we do a great deal of joint work on these problems, this help has been both general and specific; in addition I have learnt a great deal from their researches in this field. Miss Geraldine Orr has also helped me in the collection and preparation of some of the data; Miss Joan Humphreys and Miss Jacqueline Girvin have also helped in the preparation of the manuscript. My wife has done most of the typing, as well as bearing the accustomed brunt of lost evenings and weekends and the usual strains of living with the preparation of a book.

For the many faults which remain the responsibility is entirely my own.

Queen's University of Belfast,   JAMES BATES
May 1970.

CONTENTS

Preface to the First Edition   *page* v

Preface to the Second Edition   ix

List of Tables   xiii

1. THE IMPORTANCE OF SMALL BUSINESS   1
   The persistence of small business   9
   Some problems   13
   The problem of finance   14
   Some comparisons of large and small companies   17
   Summing up   21

2. THE GROWING SMALLER BUSINESS   24

3. FINANCE AND THE SMALL BUSINESS   28

4. FINANCIAL PLANNING AND CONTROL   33
   Profit planning   35
   Accounting records   36
       Financial and operating ratios   45
       Some problems in the interpretation of accounting
       records   48
   Budgets   54
       Internal financial control   58
   Break-even analysis   60
   The appraisal of capital expenditure   62
   Summing up   72

5. PROFITS AND INTERNAL FINANCE   73
   Profitability   73
   The disposal of income   78
   Other internal sources   84
       Depreciation   84
       Future tax reserves   85
       Liquid assets   86
   Self financing   87
   Company saving and the financing of small business   89

6. LONG TERM CAPITAL 92
    Private companies 92
    Going public 93
    The New Issue Market 94
    Forms of capital 95
    Renting 97
    Some specific problems 97
    Alternative sources and institutions 102
    Summing up 109

7. BANK CREDIT 112
    Bank credit and the banker 113
    Bank borrowing and the individual firm 117

8. TRADE CREDIT 122
    Trade credit in small and big business 122
    The financing of trade credit 126
    Factoring 128
    The costs of trade credit 130

9. OTHER SOURCES OF FUNDS 134
    Directors' Loans 134
    Hire-Purchase 135
    Equipment Leasing 141
    Bills of Exchange 143
    The Merchant Banks 146
    Finance for Innovations 147
    The Finance of Exports 152
    Other Government Assistance 157
    The Finance of Agriculture 159

10. MERGERS AND TAKE-OVERS 163

11. FURTHER IMPLICATIONS 167

BIBLIOGRAPHY 177

Index 183

LIST OF TABLES

1. Size of Manufacturing Establishments in Great Britain   2–3
2. Enterprises and Establishments in United Kingdom 1963   4
3. Size of Establishments in the Retail Trade in Great Britain 1961   5
4. Size of Businesses in the Wholesale Trade in Great Britain 1950   7
5. Registration of Companies with Share Capital in Great Britain   8
6. Balance Sheet Summary   18
7. Sources and Uses of Funds   19
8. Sources of Funds 1950–1956   20
9. Balance Sheet of XYZ Manufacturing Company for Year Ended March 31, 19—   38
10. Income Statement of XYZ Manufacturing Company for Year Ended March 31, 19—   40
11. Trading Account of XYZ Manufacturing Company for Year Ended March 31, 19—   42
12. Sources and Uses of Funds of XYZ Manufacturing Company for Year Ended March 31, 19—   44
13. Mr. X's Budget   56
14. Discounted Cash Flow Calculations   70
15. Costs of Various Groups of Firms 1954   74
16. Profit/Net Asset Ratios of Private Companies and Quoted Public Companies 1956   76
17. Income Net of Tax as Percentage of Net Assets   77
18. The Appropriation of Income 1956   78
19. Percentage Appropriation of Gross Income of Private, Unquoted and Quoted Public Companies, United Kingdom 1956 and 1962   83

20. Net Liquid Positions of Private, Unquoted and Quoted
     Public Companies 1956 and 1962   86

21. The Relation of Savings to Expenditure   88

22. ICFC Financial Facilities Outstanding March 31, 1969   105

23. Reasons for Not Trying Outside Sources of Funds   109

24. Analysis of Bank Advances to United Kingdom
     Residents, November 1969   114

CHAPTER 1

THE IMPORTANCE OF SMALL BUSINESS*

GIANT companies hit the headlines and dominate many sectors of British industry, and it is not surprising that they attract most of the attention of economists, politicians and financial journalists. Quoted public companies in manufacturing industry in the United Kingdom accounted, in 1951, for 46 per cent. of total employment, for about 50 per cent. of net output and for about 75 per cent. of profits (see *Bib.* 25); the proportions have changed little, but the bigger businesses probably enjoy a progressively more important role as time goes on. But it is all too easy to forget that small businesses still play an important role in the British economy, and the Radcliffe Committee (*Bib.* 72) commented in 1959:

"It is some measure of the importance of private firms in British industry that, of the total gross profits earned in manufacturing, building and distribution, less than two-thirds are taken by quoted public companies while the remaining third is earned by private and unquoted public companies."

Table 1 gives further indication of the importance of small firms in manufacturing industry: establishments employing between 11 and 499 persons accounted for 95 per cent. of total establishments and 52 per cent. of employment in manufacturing establishments employing over ten persons in Great Britain in 1961 (the proportions have remained more or less the same in recent years). To some extent this table overstates the position: an establishment is merely an address where business is carried on, and one firm may own several establishments; the net result of this is that several small establishments are branches or other parts of large firms. In fact 10,500 of these establishments are owned by quoted public companies, and an unknown number are branches of unquoted and private companies. The greater economic weight of the big concerns is shown in the preponderance of employment in firms with over 500 employees, which employ almost half of the working population of manufacturing industry.

* References to the Bibliography are indicated. *e.g.* see *Bib.* 25; the Bibliography is to be found on pages 177–181.

1

TABLE 1

SIZE OF MANUFACTURING ESTABLISHMENTS IN GREAT BRITAIN, JUNE 1961

Number of Establishments	Total	Number of Employees						Less than 100 as % of Total	Less than 500 as % of Total
		11–24	25–99	100–499	500–999	1,000–1,999	2,000 or more		
Food, drink and tobacco	5,274	1,425	2,359	1,224	153	88	28	71·7	75·9
Chemicals and allied industries	2,451	488	1,086	685	107	56	29	64·2	92·1
Metal manufacture	2,166	353	942	603	141	69	58	59·8	87·6
Engineering and electrical goods	10,684	2,285	5,166	2,427	426	249	131	69·7	92·4
Shipbuilding and marine engineering	755	180	304	173	51	31	16	64·1	87·0
Vehicles	1,931	388	810	437	120	82	94	62·0	84·7
Metal goods not elsewhere specified	5,035	1,272	2,655	931	125	43	9	77·9	96·5
Textiles	5,559	875	2,568	1,878	184	38	16	61·9	95·7
Clothing and footwear (including leather, leather goods and fur)	7,195	1,598	4,155	1,315	105	20	2	79·9	98·2
Bricks, pottery, glass, cement, etc.	2,646	541	1,412	589	65	26	13	73·8	96·1
Paper, printing and publishing	5,215	1,323	2,711	990	126	49	16	77·3	96·2
Other manufacturing industries (including timber, furniture, etc.)	6,250	1,843	3,310	961	90	29	17	82·4	97·8
TOTAL	55,161	12,571	27,478	12,213	1,693	777	429	72·6	94·7

Number of Employees (thousands)	Total	Number of Employees						Less than 100 as % of total	Less than 500 as % of total
		11–24	25–99	100–499	500–999	1,000–1,999	2,000 or more		
Food, drink and tobacco	734	25	118	266	104	119	102	19·5	55·7
Chemicals and allied industries	466	9	56	146	73	74	108	13·9	45·3
Metal manufacture	603	7	51	134	97	96	218	9·6	31·8
Engineering and electrical goods	1,985	41	268	518	298	351	509	15·6	41·7
Shipbuilding and marine engineering	192	3	16	38	37	43	55	9·9	29·7
Vehicles	854	7	41	92	84	115	515	5·6	16·4
Metal goods not elsewhere specified	514	22	136	186	86	58	26	30·7	66·9
Textiles	789	16	141	403	124	56	49	19·8	70·9
Clothing and footwear (including leather, leather goods and fur)	594	28	213	249	68	27	9	40·6	82·5
Bricks, pottery, glass, cement, etc.	321	9	75	122	45	35	35	26·2	64·2
Paper, printing and publishing	572	23	139	206	86	64	54	28·3	64·3
Other manufacturing industries (including timber, furniture, etc.)	554	32	166	192	61	40	63	35·9	70·4
TOTAL	8,178	222	1,420	2,552	1,163	1,078	1,743	20·1	51·3

Source: *Annual Abstract of Statistics*, No. 106, 1969, Table 143, p. 132.

TABLE 2

ENTERPRISES AND ESTABLISHMENTS IN UNITED KINGDOM 1963

Size of Enterprise (total number of persons employed in all industry groups)	Enterprises	Establishments	Employment	Net Output	Net Output per Head	Capital Expenditure Less Disposals	Capital Expenditure per Head
	Number	Number	Thousands	£ Million	£	£ Million	£
TOTAL—All industries	—	174,353	9,114	12,193	1,338	1,093	120
All manufacturing industries	64,367	83,774	7,695	10,470	1,361	983	128
50,000 and over	10	692	728	1,173	1,612	153	211
20,000–49,999	28	1,404	941	1,356	1,440	143	152
10,000–19,999	60	1,726	824	1,237	1,501	134	163
5,000– 9,999	112	2,209	799	1,217	1,523	116	146
2,000– 4,999	318	2,879	942	1,335	1,418	121	128
1,000– 1,999	449	2,489	630	840	1,333	70	111
500– 999	845	3,021	594	780	1,314	61	103
200– 499	2,342	4,923	725	874	1,205	67	93
100– 199	3,376	5,004	468	535	1,142	42	89
TOTAL: 100 and over	7,540	24,347	6,651	9,347	1,405	907	136
25–99	11,551	13,582	606	676	1,115	47	77
1–24	45,276	45,845	438	447	1,019	30	69

Source: 1963 *Census of Production*, No. 132, Table 13.

Table 2 distinguishes between enterprises and establishments; it shows fairly clearly that for smaller enterprises there is little difference between the establishment and the enterprise (for businesses with fewer than 100 employees enterprises are 96 per cent. of establishments, whereas for units of over 100 employees, enterprises are only 36 per cent. of establishments, and the proportion decreases as size increases). The smaller the establishment, the more likely it is to be a business unit in its own right; 90 per cent. of enterprises employ fewer than 100 persons (71 per cent. of establishments employ fewer than 100 persons); they also employ almost 14 per cent. of the working population in manufacturing industry, and account for 11 per cent. of net output and 8 per cent. of capital expenditure. Net output per head and capital expenditure per head tend to grow with increases in the size of the enterprise.

Differences between industries are also shown in Table 1. In terms of number of establishments there are few differences: there are only four industries (food, drink and tobacco, metal manufacture, shipbuilding and vehicles) in which more than 10 per cent. of establishments employ over 500 people. In terms of employment the differences are greater, and the range is from metal manufacture in which

TABLE 3

SIZE OF ESTABLISHMENTS IN THE RETAIL TRADE
IN GREAT BRITAIN 1961

	Number of Establishments	Turnover (£000)	Persons Engaged	
			Full-time	Part-time
Establishments with				
0 or 1 person engaged	113,384	367,301	94,448	12,731
2 persons engaged	140,349	965,256	208,174	72,524
3 ,, ,,	84,236	888,878	176,317	76,391
4 ,, ,,	52,599	746,069	145,383	65,013
5– 6 ,, ,,	52,425	1,022,047	197,264	85,541
7– 9 ,, ,,	30,447	872,708	167,361	69,449
10–19 ,, ,,	23,985	1,103,007	220,152	88,894
20–49 ,, ,,	8,006	846,380	179,181	52,731
50–99 ,, ,,	1,905	479,734	101,780	27,388
100 and over ,,	1,193	1,006,570	232,225	65,868
TOTAL RETAIL TRADE	508,529	8,297,949*	1,722,285	616,530
Establishments with				
Less than 10 as % of total	93·1	58·6	57·4	61·9
Less than 100 as % of total	99·8	87·9	86·5	89·3

Source: *Census of Distribution*, 1961, Part I, p. 48, Table 8 (H.M.S.O. 1963).
* Total as printed in the Census.

almost 70 per cent. of employees work in establishments with more than 500 employees, to clothing and footwear, in which less than 20 per cent. of employees work in establishments with more than 500 employees.

In the retail trade, details of which are shown in Table 3, small firms are even more important. In 1961 there were just over half a million establishments, and firms with fewer than 100 employees dominate the trade both in terms of employment and sales turnover.

In wholesaling the pattern is slightly different, with 14 per cent. of establishments in the "large" category of over £1,000,000 of sales, and 69 per cent. of sales being made by these establishments.

Further evidence of the persistence of small firms in Britain is provided by studies of the concentration of ownership in industry (see *Bib.* 32). Concentration of ownership in a trade may be measured by expressing the employment of the three largest business units in the trade as a percentage of the total employment in the trade; this may be called the *concentration ratio.* In British industry as a whole in 1951 this ratio was 29 per cent. Industries with the highest concentration ratios were: chemicals and allied trades (51 per cent.); electrical engineering and electrical goods (48 per cent.); and vehicles (41 per cent.). Industries with the lowest concentration ratios were: building, contracting and civil engineering (12 per cent.); clothing and footwear (14 per cent.); and woollen and worsted (18 per cent.). These proportions are changing over time, but the rate of change is small.

The casual observer may feel that big firms are becoming so important that small firms will count less and less in the future; it is interesting, however, that there is little evidence of increasing concentration of industry. Big firms continue to get even bigger, but, to compensate, small firms continue to exist and to set up in business.

Evely and Little distinguish three main types of British industry, which together account for 85 per cent. of total employment: most important is the *low concentration* group, in which a few large companies are surrounded by a host of small ones (the iron and steel industry before nationalisation and the manufacture of drugs are examples); next most important is the *nearly competitive* type, in which there are many firms with no extreme disparities in size (the clothing and building industries are examples); and the least important type is that in which one or more giants control more than

TABLE 4

SIZE OF BUSINESSES IN THE WHOLESALE TRADE IN GREAT BRITAIN 1950

Organisations with Sales of: (Upper Limit)	Organisations	Establishments	Receipts (£000)	Sales (£000)	Persons Engaged (000)	
					Full-time	Part-time
— £5,000	3,899	3,917	9,513	9,635	6,240	2,497
— £10,000	3,802	3,853	27,243	28,264	10,778	2,773
— £25,000	8,250	8,421	130,654	138,980	35,512	6,400
— £50,000	7,608	7,978	249,007	274,837	51,607	6,079
— £100,000	7,105	7,853	439,171	507,282	73,531	6,100
— £250,000	6,728	8,327	867,723	1,048,913	116,700	6,884
— £500,000	2,919	4,366	799,527	1,013,214	92,090	4,444
— £1,000,000	1,520	2,991	775,076	1,052,360	78,409	2,954
— £5,000,000	1,220	4,069	1,634,603	2,424,635	141,502	5,508
£5,000,000 and over	309	3,581	4,498,775	6,577,784	127,546	3,968
TOTAL, excluding warehousing	43,360	55,356	9,431,293*	13,075,250*	733,915	47,607
TOTAL, including warehousing	43,533	55,593	9,444,272	13,076,250	750,078	48,504

Source: *Census of Distribution*, 1950. Vol. III, p. 96, Table 11 (H.M.S.O. 1953).
* Totals as printed in the Census.

one-third of output, as in the motor-vehicle industry, the aircraft industry and mineral oil refining.

This is not to deny the importance of big business: the giants dominate manufacturing industry, and their actions have a tremendous impact on the economy. But it is necessary to keep the matter in perspective: the small firm still has a major contribution to make to economic life.

The small business may operate either as a public or private company, a partnership or a private individual (the two last named are referred to as "unincorporated businesses"). Numerically unincorporated businesses account for something like half of the total number of business concerns in Britain; and their income comes to about 30 per cent. of total income from all economic activities in Britain; income from companies accounts for about 55 per cent. of the total; the rest is attributable to central and local Government authorities.

Between 1949 and 1966, 444,151 companies were registered in Great Britain (see Table 5), and the rate of registration has been

TABLE 5

REGISTRATION OF COMPANIES WITH SHARE CAPITAL
IN GREAT BRITAIN

Companies Registered 1949–1966

Nominal Capital	Number of Companies
Under £1,000	239,172
£1,000– £4,999	131,933
£5,000– £9,999	35,630
£10,000–£49,999	32,709
£50,000–£99,999	2,668
£100,000 and over*	2,039
TOTAL	444,151

* Including 154 companies with nominal capital over £1 million.
Source: Companies General Annual Report by the Board of Trade for the years ended December 31, 1958, pp. 16 and 18, and December 31, 1966, p. 21.

increasing. There has been a slight move towards re-registration of private limited companies as unlimited companies since the 1967 Companies Act, which abolished exempt private company status; the effect has however been small, and private companies still account for well over 90 per cent. of the total, although they account for only about one-third of paid-up capital (see *Bib.* 22).

Outside agriculture and professional services, public and private companies are becoming increasingly important. It is these small concerns, however, which have particular problems in the field of finance, and these problems are what this book is about.

The persistence of small business

The big firm enjoys substantial advantages over the small firm. In most industries there are economies to be gained from large-scale production (the currently fashionable term is *synergy*), and these may arise in any or all of the departments of the firm (see *Bib.* 19). Technical economies may be due to the ability of large concerns to use expensive machinery capable of high rates of output at low unit cost, the large firms can also afford specialisation both of people and machines and can reap the rewards of the increased efficiency which usually goes hand in hand with such specialisation. In the fields of marketing and competition, finance, management and even risk-bearing (which may be reduced if the firm deals in large quantities or is able to diversify the scope of its activities) the same is true; indeed, the big concern gains so many advantages from large-scale operation that the dice seem heavily loaded against the small concern.

The continued existence and vitality of so many small businesses may be explained on several grounds. In the first place there are many business activities which are not suited to large-scale enterprise: bespoke tailoring is the classic example of the economics textbooks, and indeed it is frequently argued that the clothing trade as a whole is just as efficiently carried on on a small scale as on a large scale. One reason for this may be that in such trades there are not many technical economies of scale, and much of the plant and equipment used is of small output capacity; in the clothing trade the typical equipment is a sewing machine, and there is not much to be gained from the use of bigger machines; in the skilled parts of the light-engineering trade quite a lot of the equipment, although fairly expensive, is multi-purpose and does not depend on high rates of output to justify its costs. Wherever the job can be done as cheaply (per unit of output) with small machines as with large, there are not many *technical* economies of large-scale production and the existence of small firms is favoured. In some trades, too, the extent of the market may set a limit to the size of the firms: there is only a small demand for "quality" motor-cars (as it happens most of these are in fact produced by relatively small subsidiaries of big concerns operating outside the motor industry); and the demand for hardware in a particular locality may be fairly easily satisfied by one or two small firms (this has traditionally been the case in many service and distributive trades, although even in these trades there may be economies in administration, and there is an increasing tendency for large firms to own several widely dispersed branches). In such circumstances there is no point in a firm being big. As technology advances and as management techniques improve, opportunities for large-scale production arise on a wider scale, and some traditionally small-scale industries now offer prospects of larger-scale operation; but there are still many industries and trades in which small scale operation is both possible and profitable.

These are the traditional arguments for the existence of small firms, and they help to explain why some trades are predominantly small-scale, they do not, however, explain why in many industries both large and small firms exist, and the small firms are able to earn a living alongside their bigger neighbours. One reason is that the big firms frequently tolerate small competitors, who may only take an insignificant part of the market; the existence of such small firms may be put forward as an argument that the big firm is not monopolistic and that the trade is competitive. More cynically, the big firms may not yet have got around to mopping up the small firms, or may not think the effort worth while. At the price of a strictly limited degree of independence in such circumstances the small firms usually follow the leadership of the big firms and avoid making trouble: they usually know or fear that they could easily be put out of business.

This again explains only some of the cases, and there is a host of other conditions which may favour the small firm. There are frequently "external" economies which accrue to an industry or a locality as a result of large-scale operation: these may take the form of the growth of specialised ancillary trades such as the components trades surrounding the motor industry, and of special advisory services, financial intermediaries, trade associations, the provision of technical and other information, and so on. Small firms are able to take advantage of such external economies, and may benefit from the association with big firms. Big firms may not find it worth while to manufacture many of their components, usually because their own demand would not justify the large-scale production which is the principal *raison d'être* of the big firm; the small firm may take advantage of this. Steindl (see *Bib.* 79) argues that imperfect competition may favour the small firm: this is largely a technical economic argument, but it may be summed up: market imperfections may be due to such factors as advertising, resale price maintenance, the difficulty of transport over long distances and so on; and when these imperfections are found, the firm may not be able to achieve economies of scale because its own particular market may be limited. In the market in which the firm buys its materials and labour there may be special difficulties: Steindl cites the case of agricultural products, which may have to be collected over a wide area, and which lead to increasing material cost as the firm extends its scale of operations; in the case of labour, the firm may be able to get labour more cheaply outside the main industrial areas, and labour is usually less easily organised into trade unions in small firms.

Many trades are relatively easy to enter with little capital—this is particularly true of the service trades—and, whilst many of the annual crop of new entrants will regularly fail, many will succeed and survive. The desire for independence is a powerful reason why so many small firms set up, and continue even though the owners may make no better a living than they would under someone else's employment. For this reason too, many firms stay small rather than expand by bringing in partners or other outsiders; they feel that the price of expansion is too high. Similarly, a high proportion of firms are run on a family basis using the house as a place of work and vice versa, and using unpaid or underpaid family labour (underpaid in the sense that they could earn more for doing the same job outside); and such firms may well remain small from a sense of family pride and a desire to keep the firm in the family. Non-family firms, too, may wish to stay small simply because the proprietors are not strongly motivated by expansion; to many individuals there does not seem much point in seeking to expand beyond the point where a comfortable living may be earned, with a car, a house, a regular holiday, membership of a golf club and so on; the effort may not seem worth while. Tycoons may deride such individuals, and to the go-ahead businessman such behaviour may represent the extreme of folly; but regardless of such value judgments, such firms will continue to exist, and there will be just as many to wish them luck. It is of course rarely possible to stand still for long, simply because things change and the static business may slip back in relative terms; the static business is usually in decline, but the decline may be slow, and many owners of small businesses will settle for that. Many more will fail to realise that it is happening until too late; their fate is often sad.

A growing economy provides opportunities for the small firm. As the population grows and as incomes per head grow, there is an increasing demand for goods and services, and the small firms share in the satisfaction of the demand. Growth usually goes hand in hand with an increase in innovations, and many innovators are small firms. Mrs. Penrose (see *Bib.* 66) provides a further argument about the opportunities provided by growth for smaller firms. She calls these opportunities the *interstices* in the economy, and argues: 'If ... the opportunities for expansion in the economy increase at a faster rate than the large firms can take advantage of them and if the large firms cannot prevent the entry of small firms, there will be continued growth in the size and number of favourably endowed small firms.'

The small firm also has a number of specific advantages: it can frequently be more flexible in its production planning; it does not have many of the communications and human relations problems of larger, more hierarchical and bureaucratic bodies, and the personal touch of the owner-manager can help in building up team spirit and what has come to be known as the motivation of his work force. These advantages can be overstressed, but they do represent opportunities for the smaller business to reduce some of the disadvantages of smallness.

It is sometimes argued (see *Bib.* 79) that the opposite of growth—unemployment—may also result in the setting up of small firms. Men who become unemployed may set up their own firms in the attempt to survive, and this is thought to have been particularly important in the United States in the depression of the 1930s.

Finally, it should not be forgotten that many firms are small simply because they are at an early stage of their growth; such firms may well be big in twenty years' time: sixty years ago the Nuffield organisation and the Kenning organisation were both small firms. Many firms start big, but many start in a small way.

A substantial part of the explanation of the continued existence of small firms is, therefore, that they do a different job from the big firms. They are different not only quantitatively—in the numbers of employees, capital employed, volume of sales, etc.—but also qualitatively, in the composition of their output, the things they make, the markets in which they sell, and so on. To the extent to which this is so, they will continue to exist, to set up, and to make a living alongside the big firms. And in doing so they will continue to play a vital role in the functioning of trade and commerce.

Some problems

But their existence is not trouble-free. One inevitable consequence of the ease with which an individual may set up in business in many trades is the corresponding ease with which he may fail; something like 2,000 private individuals go bankrupt each year, and a further 300 to 400 companies are compulsorily liquidated, and these figures do not take account of the many firms which simply fold up quietly. All firms face risks, but they are proportionately greater the smaller the firm: the failure of a production batch in a small firm may spell disaster; a similar failure in a big organisation can frequently be predicted (the manager should have a fair idea of the probability of such occurrences), and can also be more easily absorbed.

This major risk apart there are several other problems. In some trades the inability of the small firm to achieve economies from large-scale production combined with other factors may mean that productivity is relatively low and costs accordingly high; if this cannot be recouped by higher selling prices, the small firm may have to be content with relatively low returns in the form of profits. Direct comparisons of the profitability of firms are notoriously tricky, but there is some evidence (see *Bib.* 12) that small businesses are perhaps rather less profitable than large ones.

Looking at the matter in another way, there is some evidence that in the United States at least, the average income of the *proprietors* of unincorporated businesses was not much different from that of the *employees* of all firms. The average income of business proprietors (including professional practitioners) in 1956 was $4,760, the average for full-time employees in industry was $4,100 (in transport and mining it was over $5,000) (see *Bib.* 80). This may be one of the prices paid for independence.

In the field of ownership, control and management, the small firm may have special difficulties. Death duties cause special problems in family firms, and even if this can be overcome, there are frequently difficulties in ensuring adequate succession of competent ownership and control. Management may be tricky: when the founder dies it is often found that it was his particular ability (in one form or another) which was responsible for the success of the firm; the choice of someone to succeed him may not be easy and the firm may not be prepared to pay an adequate salary to an outsider. But even in cases where no deaths or other changes of control are involved, management presents special problems for the small firm. Big firms can

employ specialist managers, and a great deal of work can be
delegated through the administrative system; in small firms, not only
are many proprietors completely unwilling to delegate but they frequently do not have anyone to whom to delegate, and the owner of a
small firm may well have to be production manager, sales manager,
personnel manager and financial manager all rolled into one. In the
very small firm this may not matter very much, though the combination of the qualities required for all of these jobs in one man is rare:
when the firm starts to grow, however, it matters a great deal, and the
inability to delegate decisions to properly qualified subordinates may
make the difference between success and failure in the attempt to
grow. Up to a certain size, control in one pair of hands is feasible;
but beyond that size the job may be too much for one man, however
good, to handle. Growth beyond that size requires a fundamental
change in the administrative structure of the firm, and this may be
beyond both the desires and capability of many small businesses.
Indeed, a small business is sometimes defined as one in which control
and effective decisions remain in the hands of one man; growth of
management beyond this stage is frequently taken as partial evidence
of ability to grow.

Although it may not be seen as a specific problem by many small
firms, domination by giant concerns may be one of the prices which
has to be paid for the illusion of independence. Small manufacturers
are often dominated by big buyers, and by big competitors on the
manufacturing side, and have to take or leave the prices offered or
ruling in the market. They are particularly vulnerable to competition,
and usually have inadequate resources with which to withstand
fierce, and sometimes unfair, competition. Advertising is usually too expensive, and frequently the only form of competition open to the small
firm is in the provision of special, or personal, service. And even if
competition is withstood, there is always the danger of a take-over.

All of these problems may be summed up as the special risks of
small firms. But there is one remaining problem, which frequently
overshadows the rest, particularly at certain stages of growth, and
that is the problem of finance. It is on this particular problem that we
shall concentrate in the remainder of this book.

The problem of finance

(Put at its crudest, the financial problem of the small firm is that of
finding funds for expansion at the right time, of the right type, and in

the right quantities, at various stages of development All firms, even
the giants of private industry and the nationalised industries, have
problems of some sort with finance; the big firms, however, have
access to sources denied to the smaller and medium-sized concerns,
and they frequently have specialised finance departments which give
them further advantages)

(The small firm has three special difficulties. In the first place it
may not be able to demonstrate its chances of success in order to
persuade potential lenders (many large firms also have this problem);
in the second place, the existing lending and financial institutions
may not cater for the special problems involved in small business
finance; and third, the businessman and his advisers may not know
how or where to get the money.)

These problems have not gone unrecognised. In 1931 the
Macmillan Committee (see *Bib.* 58) pointed to the existence of what
has come to be known as the Macmillan Gap:

"It has been represented to us that great difficulty is experienced by the
smaller and medium-sized businesses in raising the capital which they from
time to time require even when the security offered is perfectly sound. To
provide adequate machinery for raising long-dated capital in amounts not
sufficiently large for a public issue, *i.e.* amounts ranging from small sums up
to say £200,000 or more, always presents difficulties."

Almost thirty years later the Radcliffe Committee (see *Bib.* 72)
commented:

". . . there is a danger, which it is socially and economically desirable to
avoid, that the growth of small firms may be impeded because they lack
some of the facilities open to larger companies for obtaining capital."

In the years since 1931 a great deal has been done in an attempt to
fill the Macmillan Gap, but there is still room for improvement and
the special financial problems of small businesses are by no means
entirely solved. It is almost impossible in practice to distinguish
between the operational and financial difficulties of the small business, since many financial problems are due simply to the fact that
present or future expected operating efficiency is not such as to offer
attractive prospects to a potential investor. There are many small
businesses which cannot get funds simply because no one in their
right mind would dream of lending them money; at the opposite
extreme there are many small businesses which are obviously such
good bets that they find little trouble in raising capital for growth; in

between there are several businesses which could improve their operating performance, their attractiveness to outside investors and their own efficiency in the utilisation and raising of funds.

Governments have not been unaware of the problems faced by the smaller business, and they have made several efforts to meet some of them. The former Industrial Re-organisation Corporation, The National Research Development Corporation and the Export Credit Guarantees Department all attempt to deal with some aspects of the problem. And in July 1969 the President of the Board of Trade announced the appointment of an independent Committee of Inquiry, under the Chairmanship of Mr. John Bolton, into the role of small firms in the national economy and the problems confronting them.

The Committee's terms of reference are:

"To consider the role of small firms in the national economy, the facilities available to them and the problems confronting them; and to make recommendations. For the purpose of the study, a small firm might be defined broadly as one with not more than 200 employees, but this should not be regarded as a rigid definition. In the course of the study it will be necessary to examine in particular the profitability of small firms and the availability of finance. Regard should also be paid to the special functions of small firms, for example, as innovators and specialist suppliers."

As a first step the Committee prepared a preliminary list of subjects to be considered. They fell under six main heads:

(1) the importance of small firms in the economy;

(2) the services available to small firms from Government, Government-sponsored agencies and other sources;

(3) the special implications for the management and development of small firms of sources of development finance and working capital, taxation, investment grants, the operation of the Industrial Training Act of 1964, the requirements of the Factories Acts, the disclosure provisions of the Companies Acts, the requirements of industrial development and planning controls, and the statistical and other returns required by the Government;

(4) the experience of small firms, and attitudes towards them, in other countries;

(5) practical proposals which can be put to Government for improving the efficiency of small firms;

(6) any other matters of relevance.

The Committee invited views and evidence, and a large volume of evidence, comment and special pleading has been submitted to them; it has come from trade associations, the CBI, chambers of commerce, professional institutions and private individuals.

The Committee is unlikely to report before the spring of 1971; its comments and recommendations will be of tremendous significance and should help a great deal in the diagnosis and solution of this major problem.

Some comparisons of large and small companies

The original version of the author's *Financing of Small Business* contained an analysis of the financial behaviour of small business based on a survey carried out in the 1950s (referred to in this book as the Oxford Survey). Further analysis of this and other data has been carried out since and is referred to in the bibliography at the end of this book. It is not necessary to repeat these analyses in detail; instead the main conclusions and some comparisons with big companies may be summarised.

Few observers agree on the definition of a small business, and economists are constantly disagreeing over the pro's and con's of various size measures, which may range from flow concepts (such as turnover, various profit and income measures, etc.) to stock concepts (such as various asset measures, employment, etc.). Fortunately it does not much matter which size measure one chooses: some measures are less than ideal, and certain measures are undoubtedly best for certain purposes, but calculations carried out by the author on a wide variety of measures have shown that there is a high correlation between most measures across a wide range of firms in Britain and the United States (see *Bib.* 13). It probably does not matter much in practice which measure is chosen, provided that it is reasonably accurately calculated, has some relevance to the problem under discussion, and is used consistently during an investigation.

One of the most convenient measures to use is employment, and generally a small business may be defined as having fewer than 500 employees, although in fact the size distribution is such that for most purposes firms with fewer than 100 employees may be taken as representative. A reasonable cut-off point is 200 employees, which includes almost every business which has problems connected with size (it may include some with enormous assets, but they can be

TABLE 6

BALANCE SHEET SUMMARY

Percentage of Total Assets

| | 1956 | | 1962 | |
Assets	I	II	III	IV
Fixed assets	32·2	39·3	38·5	49·2
Stocks	32·1	30·2	27·2	25·1
Trade debtors	25·8	19·0	25·9	19·2
Liquid assets	9·9	11·5	8·4	6·6
TOTAL*	100·0	100·0	100·0	100·0

Capital and Liabilities				
Issued capital and reserves	65·2	67·9	53·9	63·1
Long-term debt	2·2 }	10·0	5·0	9·1
Minority interests	—		1·1	2·1
Bank loans	6·5	2·8	6·4	4·7
Directors' loans	1·3	—	—	—
Trade creditors	15·9	14·4	27·4	14·9
Others	5·9	7·0	6·2	6·1
TOTAL*	100·0	100·0	100·0	100·0

I Oxford Survey Firms 1956.
II Quoted Public Companies 1956. Source: *Economic Trends*, February 1957.
III Non-quoted Public Companies 1962. Source: *Economic Trends*, February 1965.
IV Quoted Public Companies 1962. Source: *Economic Trends*, February 1965.
 * Totals do not necessarily sum to 100 because of rounding.

readily identified and do not present a serious problem in analysis or description).

For certain purposes, particularly those of potential suppliers of capital, it is convenient to think of the small business as the one in which all effective decisions are taken by one individual; it moves into a different category when it adopts management procedures which permit delegation of decision making. That is a convenient operating definition of "small," but it is not possible to use it for broad comparisons between groups because the units cannot be identified in these terms.

The comparisons in this book are on the whole between widely disparate size groups. The small concerns referred to are mainly private companies with fewer than 100 employees and net assets of less than £250,000, in the Oxford Survey. Quoted and unquoted public companies in the comparisons typically have net assets of more than £1 million (see *Bib.* 26). Not merely do the groups differ in size, they are also different in composition, in ownership and many other economic characteristics.

Patterns of financing show interesting contrasts. Broadly there are three main sources of funds for a company: its own retained profits, long-term capital, and short- and medium-term capital, and in each of these groups, small and big businesses differ.

Tables 6 and 7 summarise the financing patterns of three groups of companies: private companies, unquoted public. companies and quoted public companies. The data are highly aggregated, and, particularly in the case of private companies, are likely to give misleading impressions. The percentages quoted should therefore be treated with reservations which are apparent from the description in the text.

The Oxford Survey also used a questionnaire to elicit information from businessmen about their sources and uses of funds in the six-year period preceding the date of the interview. Information about frequency of use with no data about weight of finance must be treated with caution—for example, although share issues were rare and

TABLE 7

SOURCES AND USES OF FUNDS

| | Percentage of Total Sources/Uses | | | |
| | 1956 | | Average 1960–1962 | |
Sources of Funds	I	II	III	IV
Issued capital	33·4[1]	16·9	7·8	26·2
Depreciation provisions	34·3	24·8	27·1	27·8
Additions to future tax reserves	−9·5	3·2	−0·4	−0·3
Retained profits	44·7	32·4	21·9	23·1
Bank loans	−3·9	0·4	9·2	6·1
Directors' loans	1·6	—	—	—
Trade credit received	−16·6	12·0	28·3	10·6
Others	16·0	10·3	6·1	5·7
TOTAL*	100·0	100·0	100·0	100·0
Uses of Funds				
Expenditure on fixed assets	71·8	54·5	53·9	57·2
Increase in stocks	−25·6	16·3	22·5	15·6
Trade credit granted	37·0	16·2	20·7	13·0
Expenditure on subsidiaries }	0·2	6·1	5·2	15·8
Other capital payments			0·7	2·2
Increase/decrease in liquid assets	16·6	6·9	−3·0	−3·8
TOTAL	100·0	100·0	100·0	100·0

[1] This total is inflated by large issues by three companies.
Note: Column reference numbers as in Table 6.
* Totals do not necessarily sum to 100 because of rounding.

TABLE 8

SOURCES OF FUNDS 1950–1956

Source	Number of Firms Using Sources
A. *Ploughed back profits*	
None at all	29
1–3 years	39
4 or 5 years	77
6 years	176
Not ascertained	14
TOTAL	335
B. *Overdraft*	
None at all	162
1–3 years	49
4–6 years	121
Not ascertained	3
TOTAL	335
Duration of overdraft	
Up to 6 months	143
6–12 months	27
TOTAL	170
C. *Other Sources*	
New shares issued [1]:	
to existing shareholders	35
to outsiders	16
Debentures:	
to shareholders	3
to outsiders	7
Loans from directors	76
Loans from parent company [2]	15
Loans from building societies	20
Loans from other institutions	17
Other loans and credits	9
Hire purchase of plant and equipment	108
No other sources used in period	193
Total other sources [3]	499

[1] This includes transfers of personal capital in the case of unincorporated business.
[2] Including companies entirely financed by parent company.
[3] Since these sources are not mutually exclusive the number of sources used exceeds the number of firms in the sample.
Source: Oxford Survey.

directors' loans were frequent, the total weight of funds raised by the former method would be expected to be much greater and in some senses much more significant—but it is interesting to know how often firms use various sources since it gives an idea of the accessibility of these sources.

An overall picture is given in Table 8. Half of the firms ploughed

rely a great deal on finance from the banks: some never borrow, and many borrow only seasonally: but to those who borrow, bank loans are a very important source of funds. Bank loans are more important in private than public companies. Trade credit similarly is also more important—both as a source and as use of funds—to small firms than to quoted public companies. There is a tendency for many small firms to receive more credit than they give and to finance part of their development by these means. Directors' loans, never used by public companies, are frequently used by private companies, and although in weight they are rarely important they are frequently of great strategic significance. Hire-purchase is a frequently used and important source of funds in small firms, and is hardly ever used by public companies. Within the Oxford Survey sample the heaviest dependence of short- and medium-term borrowing was in the smaller, rapidly growing firms. In general, the larger the firm the less it tends to depend on short- and medium-term funds and the more it can finance its needs from its own resources and long-term capital.

12. The majority of small businesses are, by any reasonable definition, family firms. Broadly it is probably true that family firms rely more on internal and family sources than do non-family firms: this, however, is probably as much a function of size as of ownership. Perhaps the only behaviour characteristics directly influenced by ownership and control are those which are intuitively obvious: payment of directors' remuneration; profit retention and distribution; participation in and refusal to relinquish equity, and the consequent use of uncommitted short-term debt would be all expected and are in fact observed.

(In general small private companies find it relatively difficult to obtain funds for expansion and are frequently put in the position where they have to raise money from short- and medium-term sources at relatively high cost.)

CHAPTER 2

THE GROWING SMALLER BUSINESS

THIS book is largely concerned with the financing of the growing smaller business, whose life story might go somewhat as follows.

Setting up in business on one's own is not terribly difficult, although it may require an uncommon kind of courage or self-confidence. Many who set up on their own are destined to remain small, and are content to do so: the plumber, the small shopkeeper, the odd-job man, the small contractor and the like are frequently content with their lot, have little wish to grow beyond their present size and perform a useful service in the community. They have financial problems, particularly in the early stages, or when they are experiencing severe competition from newcomers, but many of them are problems of survival rather than finance as such; others may be problems of internal financial control such as collection of debts, size of stocks and so on. Real though these problems are, they are not the main concern of this book. One of the main problems of such a business is keeping the customer content and the books balanced.

There is another type of small entrepreneur. He is the man who sets up on his own because, for example, he has a process or a skill to exploit, or because he identifies a niche in the market in which he sees opportunities for profit. He may have very little capital in the first instance, and he may well be content to work for a relatively small return in the early stages. But he wants to grow, and as he succeeds in this aim his needs for funds increase. Some of this need he can meet from retained profits, some he may have to meet by borrowing from his creditors; but he will need the money simply in order to expand his sales, regardless of whether he needs to buy more plant and equipment. To the horror of many, he may well over-trade, putting himself in the position where he could not pay his creditors; bad though this is as a long-term thing, he may well be forced to do it, and his creditors may well be prepared to let him do so within limits. Unfortunately many a small enterprise has gone on the rocks at this stage, simply because the businessman, unwise in the ways of business, has allowed himself to be persuaded that just because a sale is profitable, it will also bring in the money at the right time (in the jargon, he fails to budget and to think in terms of the cash flow which he will need to pay his suppliers, his workpeople and himself).

Frequently in the early stages of a business such as this there is little point in looking for outside funds (if the entrepreneur is an innovator or has a technological breakthrough with a potentially good market he may be in a position to do so, but he is a special case); the reason simply is that there may be little to back other than the man, who has yet to prove himself, and few financiers are indiscriminate philanthropists.

But he may wish to grow further and faster. He may want to buy more equipment, or to increase his labour force, or extend his premises, or spend on advertising or any of a number of things which he has not done before and which place new demands on his financial resources. At this stage he may go to a hire-purchase finance company for finance for his plant, or he may try to rent premises, or he may go to his bank and ask for accommodation. At this stage his potential backers are going to want to know a bit more about his finances; they may be pretty severe on over-trading; they will certainly need some evidence or prospect of stability; they may ask him to put more money into the business himself. But they may help him out. A traditional source at this stage is the private individual backer with sufficient faith to back the entrepreneur with a thousand pounds or so. Such private backers are unfortunately less easy to find than they were, but there are still some.

In time he will need more capital if he is to grow further. The bank may be unable to help since he may require long-term capital; his needs may be inappropriate to hire purchase or leasing, and he may be looking for longer-term help. At this stage he is really going to have to let other people into his affairs; he may go to one of the specialist institutions, or to a merchant bank, or an insurance company or a similar institution. At this stage he is going to have to demonstrate fairly conclusively that he is worth backing. He may well have to form a company, normally a private one in the first instance, and he is going to have to start taking matters of finance and management much more seriously (in the sense of learning about them) than was necessary in the past. In a sense any business which has got this far has had some success and is better than average, but the lender wants rather more and is really asking why the businessman may be expected to continue to succeed in the higher league to which he aspires.

If he is taken up by a specialist institution his financial worries may well be over at this stage, although many of his other worries will just be starting. But he may well get past this stage without the need to go to a specialist institution; he may, for example, find a partner or someone willing to back him.

But if he does get past this stage he runs into other problems. Some of these are financial—he still needs to finance his growing sales and his accounts receivable for example, and his materials and labour still need to be paid for well in advance of any payment for the goods or services which he may sell—others are managerial. The managerial problems arise because the business is getting too big for one man to run; he may have to employ a salesman, or an accountant, or an engineer or a works manager, depending on what he is himself and what the needs of his business are. His organisation is becoming too big for him to supervise everything directly, but he may well take all the major decisions.

If he needs further funds at this stage, potential lenders are going to look at other things besides his balance sheet. They are going to want to know whether his organisation can grow to meet the needs of further expansion, and they are going to want to know a great deal more about the market.

This is the stage which really decides whether the business remains small. If in future all of the major decisions are still going to be taken by one man the likelihood is that it will remain small (or at any rate that outside money will not be forthcoming); if the organisation can develop, however, so that it can cope managerially with growth, it could grow. And provided that management is capable of growing with the business, there is no long-term limit (although it may take quite a time to get as far as the entrepreneur wishes).

That is a very simple story of growth; it is, however, a fairly common one, and it is one which carries with it many problems of financing. The object of this book is simply to identify these problems and to illustrate and demonstrate ways in which they may be met. It gives simple guidelines and little more; it is not a text for the big business, neither is it a series of recipes designed to help the business in severe financial difficulties (there are neither principles nor institutions which alone can save the sinking ship; neither is anyone likely to come forward to make its last moments more comfortable or to keep it afloat for a little longer in the hope that things may improve). There may be a book to be written for the business in such circumstances, but this is not it: the need goes far beyond normal company doctoring, which can only rescue the business if it is reasonably well founded on a product, a market or a management or some other potentially profitable asset.

It is glib to say so, but prevention is better than cure; this book is about planning and prevention and not about cure.

CHAPTER 3

FINANCE AND THE SMALL BUSINESS

(SMALL businesses have particular problems in the field of finance, and in many ways these are very different from the financial problems of large concerns. But the principles underlying any financial decision are similar whatever the size of the business.)

Many of the so-called financial problems of small businesses are merely reflections of general managerial problems; many owners of small businesses would be well advised to spend some time on these problems. Financial management is merely one part of overall management, albeit a very important one; time given to it can frequently reduce financial problems to manageable dimensions.

There is no single ideal way of financing a firm. Each business has individual circumstances which make its requirements unique: the industry and markets in which it operates, its age and the stage of its life-cycle which it has reached, its ownership; the rate at which its owners wish to expand, these and a whole series of other factors mean that each decision about finance has to be made in the light of the particular circumstances of each case. But there are some basic principles.

Five main considerations govern fund-raising policy:

(1) how much money is needed;
(2) when it is needed;
(3) the purposes for which it is needed;
(4) the form of finance to be used;
(5) whether it is profitable to undertake the expenditure.

The decisions will not necessarily be made in this order, but it is convenient to consider them in this way.

The amount of money required is often not easy to estimate with accuracy, but the chances of making a major mistake are reduced by budgeting and forward planning. Over-estimation of requirements is on the whole less serious than under-estimation: the former may cost the firm more in interest payments on borrowed funds which are not earning their keep; the latter may result in the firm running short of funds before returns start coming back from expenditure, and this is

28

undesirable not merely because of the immediate financial embarrassment in itself but also because it may mean that the firm finds it difficult at such a late stage to get the necessary funds to help it out of the embarrassment.

Timing too is usually a matter of planning in advance: capital equipment usually needs to be ordered a long time ahead, and even when it arrives in the factory it may take some time to install and reach the stage where its operations yield a profit to the firm. In extreme cases, such as the sinking of a coal-mine or the building of a steelworks the process may take several years, but even relatively small items may take several months; and whatever the period, finance has to be found to bridge it.

The form of finance to be used will depend partly on this time factor, and partly on the uses to which the money will be put. Broadly the firm has three main sources from which it may raise funds for day-to-day operation and for expansion. *Internal funds* are derived mainly from the savings of the firm from its own past profits; *long-term external funds* are raised in the form of loan or share capital; *short- and medium-term external funds* may come from a variety of sources, in the form of bank credit, hire-purchase and similar short- to medium-term obligations. These are examined in detail in subsequent chapters. There is a fourth aspect of finance, the allocation of available funds through the use of *budgets* and *internal financial control*: this is in some senses a separate problem, which is examined shortly; it is a fundamental part of the process of financing the firm and may indeed largely determine the form and the timing of fund-raising.

If the funds are merely to be used for the maintenance of existing business, internal funds will usually be sufficient, although allowance has to be made for the rising prices of equipment, materials and labour, and it is always desirable to keep a little extra in any case for eventualities. In addition such special requirements as safety, welfare, fringe benefits and so on have to be catered for. If the funds are required for expansion the decision will be more complex.

Long-term capital, whether internally or externally raised, is usually required for the finance of buildings, heavy plant and equipment, and for all large-scale extensions of productive capacity. In the long run such capital expenditure must be expected to pay for itself out of the returns earned by the operation of the plant: how long this will take in practice depends on the nature of the expenditure (it is by no means unknown for experimental plant to be expected to pay for itself within a year, but power stations, ships, steelworks and coalmines may be allowed ten years or more). Such capital should preferably be permanent, or at the very least of such a long term that it cannot be withdrawn or repaid before the plant has started to pay for itself.

In practice the small business may well have to provide such long-term capital almost entirely from its own resources, since share and loan capital may be hard to come by. In a limited number of cases specialised institutions may be able to help.

It is sometimes convenient also to finance less durable plant and equipment from long-term sources as part of one major operation involving durable plant as the principal item, thus bringing all finance into one long-term capital budget. But generally, plant of a less durable nature, such as machine tools, motor vehicles, contractors' plant and so on, which can be written off over a period of not more than five years (as a general rule) is best financed by medium-term funds. Similarly the financing of the sale of capital goods, particularly in the export market, may be undertaken from such funds, as may the financing of a fairly long-term contract such as factory or road building. There are institutions which specialise in the provision of medium-term finance and some, such as plant-leasing companies and hire-purchase finance companies, are particularly useful to the small firm; but in this field as in others, the small firm has its peculiar difficulties.

Short-term funds—of which bank credit is overwhelmingly the most important—are usually best suited to debt which is self-liquidating (*i.e.* it very soon pays for itself). Production time-lags, such as that of the farmer who has to pay for his seed six months before the harvesting and sale of his crop are frequently financed in this way, as are short-term contracts of all kinds. Seasonal stock peaks such as occur in firms which manufacture in the winter months for sale in the summer, and the regular monthly or quarterly payment of accounts owing to creditors may also be financed in this way. In general this is the field of external finance in which the small established firm has least difficulty; but even here the growing firm may not find it particularly easy to finance an expansion of turnover.

Other considerations may affect the form of finance. The legal form of a business may have a major bearing on what is possible and desirable. Initially the unincorporated business relies for its long-term capital on the contribution of partners or the sole owner plus a limited amount of private borrowing; later it may use its retained profits, or borrow from the bank, or other partners may be brought in. But there is usually a limit to the extent to which these courses are possible, and the unincorporated business may be unable to raise extra funds. It is unusual for example to find an unincorporated business with much long-term loan capital. A change of legal form to company status, and the issue of share capital is frequently a way out of such a difficulty. The private company can always issue shares if it wishes to raise capital but the amount which it can raise in this way may be severely restricted; such a company may become a public company, and if a quoted public company it can use the resources and contacts of the capital market and can command proportionately much larger resources. Such changes of legal form may well be a useful way of raising funds if the circumstances are right, since they allow the firm to tap new sources of finance; however, circumstances do not always favour this course of action.

The existing structure of ownership of the firm may impose limitations. Some forms of finance, notably ordinary share capital, constitute a form of ownership, and the firm which attempts to raise funds in this way may have to face the risk that some degree of ownership and control (via voting rights) may have to go to outsiders. This may well be acceptable as one of the costs of growth, but many owners of small firms are reluctant to let any share of their business leave their own hands; since few lenders of long-term capital are prepared to put money into a small and possibly little-known firm without some say in the running of the business, the price of such independence may well be a failure to grow.

Reluctance to share ownership with outsiders may of course go hand in hand with a desire to borrow money; the cost of debt may appear to be lower when account is taken of the fact that interest on it qualifies for tax relief, and it does not imperil ownership. But the *debt versus equity* problem, as it is known, is not a simple one. Too much debt raises a gearing problem, since fixed interest payments may take too big a slice out of the profits; debt-free companies may attract more new venture capital when it is needed; and owners might ask the question—is it better to have a partial interest in a company which has grown rather than complete control of one which has not grown so much?

One other general consideration needs to be borne in mind.

Certain forms of finance may impair liquidity, or the ability of the business to settle its current debts in cash at short notice, or may be subject to withdrawal at short notice, with similar effects. The need to pay trade creditors, or the need to make regular payments on rental or hire-purchase agreements may find the business periodically short of cash. This is largely a problem of budgeting, but it is a distressingly common stumbling-block for the small firm which is trying to expand its activities.

CHAPTER 4

FINANCIAL PLANNING AND CONTROL*

THE literature of management contains a great deal on financial planning and control; it is possible to construct elaborate procedures and descriptions, which become more and more complex the greater the ambition of their progenitor and the less clearly he sees his objectives. Much of it is simply grandiose, and for the majority of small businesses an elaborate apparatus is much less necessary than a clear understanding of the main considerations involved.

It is possible to distinguish a number of guidelines.

The first essential is to know where the owners of the business wish it to go in the next few years; this is known in the jargon as the specification of objectives and the drawing up of the long-range plan.

The owners and managers of many small businesses do not really know what their objectives are: they may have a vague general notion about maximising profit, or a sound rate of growth, or the provision of a service to the public, but they rarely spell out exactly what they mean. It is a healthy exercise, even for the smallest one-man business, to ask what one is really after in running this business. Is it a comfortable standard of living, or increasing profit, or growth of the business and one's capital, or the desire to become a tycoon, or what? There are many entrepreneurs who simply like to make things grow—they are frequently called dynamic, or go-ahead—but there are many, particularly among those who have inherited a business, who are content to jog along without the tribulations of growth. The latter group is unlikely to make a long-term success of business, because it is not easy to remain static and make a living in a changing world; if they recognise their objectives, however, there is no reason why, with elementary prudence, the maintenance of efficiency and the ability to look after their customers, they should not continue. They do not need long-term plans or any complicated apparatus, and their financial needs may be adequately met by the retention of a small amount of profit, a bit of bank borrowing and internal financial control of such items as stocks and debtors.

---

* References to the Bibliography are indicated, *e.g.* see *Bib.* 25; the Bibliography is to be found on pages 177–181.

But growth or development has other implications, and successful growth is more likely to be achieved if some sort of planning is carried out. Similarly, the small business setting up from scratch is usually more likely to succeed if it has reasonably stated objectives and plans.

The major requirements for planning and control are (see *Bib*. 19):

(*a*) the setting of objectives;

(*b*) the preparation of a plan for attaining the objectives;

(*c*) the checking of achievement of objectives and deviations from plan;

(*d*) establishment of the causes of deviation;

(*e*) remedial action, or changes of plan.

The setting of objectives is a relatively straightforward business provided that a few basic rules are borne in mind: the most important of these are that the objectives should be precisely stated, measurable and consistent. Thus, for example, it is little use to say that the objective of the business is to show a healthy growth rate. What is healthy? What is profitable? How are we to measure whether we achieve this objective? Statements such as "the maximisation of net present value" look much better but have little more meaning because they are vague, suggest no criteria and do not have any time scale. Neither is it of much value to say that the business should expand its sales by 10 per cent. per annum; that may be easily achieved and checked, but the price of it may be excessive expenditure on promotion, or overtrading, and that may not be really what is needed. The more vague are the objectives the less easy is it to draw up a plan.

The businessman may genuinely not know what his growth aims are, other than that he wants to get bigger; unfortunately he is unlikely to get bigger and make a profit at the same time unless he does draw up some concrete plans.

There is one more general precept before getting down to the detail. The vital thing on the financial side of the business is to plan and forecast the cash flow. Money is always going to flow out of the business in the payment of bills, wages, rent and so on; in order to meet these outflows, inflows are necessary. However profitable the business, if the cash inflow cannot meet the cash outflow in both the short run and the long run, trouble is not very far away; in a growing business the cash flows out a long time before anything starts to come in, and the gap has to be bridged.

This is not to say that profit does not matter, although unfortunately one might deduce this from some of the literature on the subject. Cash-flow planning always has the ultimate constraint that the business must be profitable. Contemporary emphasis on cash flows is merely an attempt to get away from unhealthy preoccupation with accounting statements of profit and loss.

Profit Planning

Profit planning in its broadest sense means nothing more than meeting the expectations or requirements of the owners of the business; in any company these are the shareholders; in the private company they are normally the directors. Profit planning for the large company consists of attempting to meet the requirements of shareholders through dividends and capital appreciation; in the smaller business neither of these may be important in the short run although they may turn out to be vital in the longer period, and in particular when outside funds are sought. Big companies frequently have detailed schemes for profit planning; such schemes are rarely feasible for smaller businesses, but fortunately they are not essential.

The main requirements of profit planning are fairly simple. They are:

(*a*) accounting records, including balance sheets, income statements and cash flow statements;

(*b*) budgets and projected cash flow statements, including budgets for both current and capital items;

(*c*) simple break-even analysis;

(*d*) business sense and judgment (without which none of the rest will get the businessman very far).

One of the first requirements for good planning is good information, and a convenient starting-point is the financial information about the business, which is normally kept in the form of accounting records.

Many owners of small businesses are horrified by accounts of any sort, because they rarely seem to tell them very much and hardly ever seem to have much relevance to current operations. The terminology of the accountant is precise and meaningful to the profession, but it is frequently obscure and misleading to the layman, and many owners of small businesses are simply over-awed.

But accounts are fairly simple things in principle, although they require detailed work in preparation; few owners of small businesses could or should prepare their own accounts, but they should try to understand them.

In simple terms the businessman wants to know from his accounting records a number of things about his present position:

(*a*) what he is worth (*i.e.* the difference between what he owns —his assets, and what he owes—his liabilities);

(*b*) whether he is solvent (*i.e.* whether he can meet his short term liabilities from his readily realisable assets);

(*c*) whether he has been making a profit (*i.e.* the difference between his costs and the revenue acquired from his sales);

(*d*) what he has been doing with the profit (*i.e.* how much he has been putting by to maintain his assets, how much for the tax man, how much for the owners of the business, and how much for growth and security);

(*e*) how his money has been raised and used (*i.e.* the cash flows in the business).

He will also want to know how he expects or plans that all of these things should go in the future.

For information about the present position he will use his historical accounting records; for information about the future he will use forecasting and planning documents and budgets. Although both sets of information relate to each other, it is convenient to separate them for purposes of discussion.

Accounting Records

The main historical records useful for financial analysis are:

(*a*) the balance sheet;
(*b*) the trading account;
(*c*) the profit and loss account (or income statement);
(*d*) the statement of sources and uses of funds.

Historical accounts come in a variety of forms, and it is up to the businessman and his financial adviser to choose a form which best suits the needs of the particular business. Accounts are frequently criticised as being designed to conceal more than they reveal, and there is some truth in the criticism as far as published accounts are concerned; for the small business in particular, however, the main purpose of accounting information is to tell the businessman what is going on and to act as a guide for the future, and the more meaningful and informative the accounts the better.

For purposes of illustration a set of standardised accounts is used in this section; they are based on actual accounts of a number of small businesses in the Oxford Survey, which were summarised in the first edition of this book, and are so designed to present the information in a relatively simple way.

The balance sheet (Table 9) is no more than a simple snapshot of the liabilities and assets of the business at any one time. In practice figures are usually shown for two financial years; this enables the reader to make comparisons between the two snapshots, but unfortunately it does not permit the reader to tell very much about what happened to actual cash flows in the period and it does not therefore explain differences between two snapshots. For example, a difference of (say) £20,000 between issued capital in two different years may simply be due to a bonus issue of shares or to a capitalisation of reserves, which did not yield any cash to the company. For this reason in the worked example given, figures for the previous year are not included, since they would not in themselves permit the sources and uses of funds to be calculated, and may confuse the reader in attempting to understand the income statements and sources and uses of funds statements.

On the capital, reserves and liabilities side it is usually convenient to distinguish between:

(a) liability for the share capital;
(b) liability for reserves accumulated over the lifetime of the business;
(c) long-term debt;
(d) current liabilities.

The first two items frequently puzzle the layman. It may seem odd that the money which has been put up by the shareholders is a liability at all; it is so only in the sense that if the company were wound up, the remaining value of assets (after paying off creditors and long-term debtors) belongs to shareholders, and part of the assets is therefore interpreted as a liability to shareholders. Similarly the

TABLE 9

BALANCE SHEET OF XYZ MANUFACTURING COMPANY FOR YEAR ENDED MARCH 31, 19—

CAPITAL, RESERVES AND LIABILITIES	£	£
Ordinary shares	19,827	
Preference shares	5,924	
ISSUED CAPITAL		25,751
Reserves and provisions	33,916	
Future tax reserves	3,896	
		37,812
TOTAL CAPITAL AND RESERVES		63,563
Long-term liabilities	2,163	
Bank loans	6,314	
Directors' loans	1,247	
Trade creditors	18,452	
Other liabilities:		
Dividends and interest	1,536	
Current taxation	33,448	
Others	823	
		33,983
TOTAL CAPITAL, RESERVES AND LIABILITIES		97,546

ASSETS	£	£
Land and buildings	11,122	
Plant and machinery	12,110	
Other fixed assets	1,293	
TANGIBLE ASSETS		24,525
Intangible assets (goodwill, etc.)	417	
Trade investments	6,440	
		6,857
FIXED ASSETS		31,382
Stocks	31,327	
Trade debtors	25,160	
Marketable securities	1,150	
Tax reserve certificates	987	
Cash	7,540	
CURRENT ASSETS		66,164
TOTAL ASSETS		97,546

Note: Accumulated depreciation on fixed assets, 13,283.

reserves of the business are part of the owners' capital in the business and are to be treated as liabilities in the same way. Issued capital and reserves are frequently referred to nowadays as the net worth or net assets of the business, because they represent the difference between the total assets of the company and what is owed to people outside the business (creditors, bankers and so on). This is analogous to the position of the private individual, who may own assets such as a car, house, furniture, cash, securities and so on, but who, if he is realistic about things, knows that he also owes some money, perhaps to the bank, or to the tax man, or to tradespeople supplying on monthly accounts, or on hire purchase, or to the building society and so on; his true, or net asset position can only be determined if he deducts these debts from his assets.

The real distinction is that the company, as a business entity, has a liability to the owners, as private individuals, for the share capital and reserves which are therefore assets of the owners.

The term *reserves* may also be misleading, and many a small business owner has asked his accountant why he cannot finance his expansion from the reserves shown on his balance sheet. The truth of the matter very simply is that the reserves figure simply shows the accumulated totals which have been put into the business in the past via retained earnings; these sums have usually been spent on the acquisition of assets, and the reserves simply do not exist in any realisable form. To find out what does exist in realisable form it is necessary to look at the assets side of the balance sheet in conjunction with the liabilities side.

Other liabilities include amounts owed to the bank, to creditors (who are frequently the suppliers, but who may also include employees who are owed money), to shareholders (in the shape of dividends due but not yet paid) and to the Inland Revenue (in the shape of taxes due but not yet paid). These are all best thought of as amounts payable by the company in the short period. The only other liability in most balance sheets is long-term debt, in the form of mortgages or debentures outstanding.

In the specimen accounts capital and reserves account for about two-thirds of the total book value of assets of the company, the remainder being owed on long and short term to outsiders.

On the assets side it is normal to show fixed assets first; these are usually in the form of land and buildings and plant and machinery, shown at written-down book values (*i.e.* original cost less

accumulated depreciation to the date of the balance sheet). As is
shown later (p. 49) these are usually shown in small business accounts as historical costs less depreciation, and the values in the
balance sheet may not be in any sense true or realistic expressions
of the value of the assets. The other assets of the company usually
include: the stocks (materials, work in progress and finished stock)
of the business as valued at the balance sheet date; the amounts
owed to the company by debtors; cash at the bank and in hand;
marketable securities; tax reserve certificates; in some businesses
there will also be trade investments. All of these current assets represent things which the company owns (or is owed) and which could
be realised. They cannot always be realised at the values shown in
the balance sheet particularly when some time has elapsed between
the drawing up of the balance sheet and the date of realisation; for
example, the stocks may by then not be correctly valued, and, of
course, marketable securities can only be sold at market prices. It
may also be found that some of the debts must now be considered as
bad debts.

In any case, as is discussed later, the company needs to keep some
of its assets to cover short-term liabilities.

TABLE 10

INCOME STATEMENT OF XYZ MANUFACTURING COMPANY FOR YEAR
ENDED MARCH 31, 19—.

	£
TRADING PROFIT (after charging interest payable)	8,622
Less Provision for depreciation	1,917
Operating Profit	6,705
Plus Other income	1,118
INCOME TO BE APPROPRIATED	7,823
Less Tax	3,905
DISPOSABLE INCOME	3,918
Less Dividends	
on ordinary shares	1,298
on preference shares	147
RETAINED PROFIT	2,473
Plus Prior year adjustments (tax, etc.)	440
TRANSFERS TO RESERVES AND PROVISIONS	2,913
Note: Directors' Remuneration	3,475

The balance sheet is then nothing more than a simple statement of what the assets and liabilities of a company look like at one chosen date in the year. In its straightforward form it can tell the owner a great deal about his financial status; it can also be used for the calculation of a number of ratios, which are discussed later. But on its own it gives at best an incomplete picture.

The income statement (Table 10) goes part of the way to explaining some of the activities which produced the results shown in the balance sheet in that it covers the time between two successive balance sheets. It shows what profits were made, how much of the profit was paid out in the form of tax, dividends and directors' fees, and how much was retained in the business; it also shows how much was put by in the form of depreciation allowances to make good wear and tear and obsolescence of assets. But the account explains only one item which is directly reflected in the balance sheet (change in reserves), and the explanation of other variations must come from elsewhere.

Underlying the income statement is the trading and profit loss account of the company (Table 11), which is shown in the example in serial form rather than in the double entry form which so many businessmen find confusing. The main items in the account are:

(*a*) cost of materials, or cost of goods, which is a simple calculation based on opening stock of the company, to which are added purchases made during the year and from which are deducted the closing stock; this simply shows how much the materials used in the business have cost during the year;

(*b*) wages and salaries;

(*c*) the other costs of the business (frequently described as its overhead costs, but which may in fact include some variable or semi-variable costs, such as packing, carriage, etc.).

The total of these items, when deducted from sales revenue, produces the figure for operating profit, which is taken to the income statement, or appropriation account.

One item which is deducible from the trading account, but which is rarely identified or used in practice, is net output, or value added; this represents the addition of value to materials by the processes of production or distribution (*i.e.* by the activities of the business); it is the real cost of the business operation in the sense that it represents the cost of transforming incoming materials or goods into saleable

TABLE 11

TRADING ACCOUNT OF XYZ MANUFACTURING COMPANY
FOR YEAR ENDING MARCH 31, 19—.

	£	£	£
NET SALES:			53,103
Opening stock	10,329		
Plus Purchases	13,174		
Less Closing stock	10,592		
COST OF STOCK		12,911	
WAGES		21,234	
SALARIES		2,020	
OTHER COSTS:			
Fuel and power	2,376		
Rent and rates	1,949		
Advertising	491		
Repairs	104		
Carriage	1,310		
Packing	161		
Insurance	215		
Stationery	365		
Travel	150		
Cleaning	165		
Telephone, postage	201		
Legal expenses	247		
Audit fee	63		
Interest	120		
Bad debts written off	150		
Sundry	249		
TOTAL OTHER COSTS		8,316	
DEPRECIATION		1,917	
TOTAL COSTS			46,398
OPERATING PROFIT (Net Sales *less* Total Costs)			6,705

commodities or services. Value added per man is a reasonable measure of the efficiency of the use of manpower, and other efficiency measures may be calculated on a similar basis.

Accounting definitions are frequently confusing, and the accountants' definition of gross profit often bewilders businessmen, since it describes gross profit as the excess of sales (less returns) over the cost of goods sold (or cost of materials); it is in a sense the gross margin of the business, or the difference between sales and some direct costs. This is not really profit at all, since it contains a large number of items which still have to be paid for. Net profit is the surplus which remains after charging against gross profit all of the other costs, including depreciation, of the business. In the accounts shown, the accountants' gross profit is probably the difference between total costs and costs of goods, plus part of wages directly attributable to putting the goods in saleable condition; net profit is sales less total costs. Net profit is a useful figure for the businessman; gross profit is a convenient figure for the accountant to calculate, but little else, since it does not really provide the businessman with much information about the costs of his business in the past and is of little help to him in planning for the future although it may be of some help in the preparation of break-even charts. What is much more important is to be able to calculate value added (which is fairly easy) and to be able to draw a distinction between fixed and variable costs, which is very difficult indeed from most conventional accounts.

The trading and profit loss account therefore produces the figures underlying the income statement; the income statement shown as Table 10 is drawn up in order to show the genuine amount of funds put to reserves as a transfer. It is, in that sense, a part of the flow of funds statement, with which it is reconciled in the sense that the £2,473 shown in the income statement as retained profit is also shown as retained profit in the flow of funds statement.

The flow of funds statement (Table 12) is also represented in simplified form. The Companies Act 1967 requires that all published accounts should show figures for current and preceding years; it may appear from this that all that is necessary for the calculation of flows of funds is to calculate the first differences between successive items, but this can give very misleading results. The actual calculation of funds flow statements is by no means simple: it is necessary to distinguish between real cash flows and book-keeping entries. For example, a bonus issue of shares, whilst it has no effect whatever on cash flows, and certainly raised no money, shows up as a change in share capital if appropriate adjustments are not made; revaluation of assets similarly does not produce any cash inflow or outflow, but again shows up as a change if unadjusted first differences are calculated. The Companies Act 1967 does not require published accounts to show sources and dispositions of funds; the proper calculations need to be made by the user.

Several methods of presentation are possible; the specimen merely shows sources and uses of funds in the simplest terms, but it might be desirable for example to identify net changes in trade credit given or received, or to show specifically how changes in net worth or operating assets were financed, or to show how the cash position at the

TABLE 12

SOURCES AND USES OF FUNDS OF XYZ MANUFACTURING COMPANY FOR YEAR ENDED MARCH 31, 19—.

SOURCES	£	£
Issue of:		
Ordinary shares	1,113	
Preference shares	12	
Long-term liabilities	725	
CAPITAL ISSUED		1,850
Increase in loans:		
From banks	−218	
From directors	86	
Decrease in amounts due to trade creditors	−919	
Additions to accruals:		
Dividends and interest	184	
Tax	−125	
Reductions in other liabilities	−48	
DECREASE IN CREDIT RECEIVED		−1,042
Retained profit	2,473	
Depreciation provisions	1,917	
Reduction in future tax reserves	−540	
ADDITIONS TO RESERVES		3,850
Other capital receipts and profits	886	
TOTAL		5,546

USES	£	£
Gross expenditure on:		
Tangible fixed assets	2,686	
Intangible assets	−32	
Trade investments	1,328	
Decrease in value of stocks	−1,420	
Increase in debtors	2,046	
Other capital payments	13	
EXPENDITURE ON OPERATING ASSETS		4,621
Increases in holdings of:		
Marketable securities	86	
Tax reserve certificates	293	
Cash	546	
INCREASE IN LIQUID ASSETS		925
TOTAL		5,546

beginning and end of the balance sheet periods changed and for what reasons. Exactly how it is done depends on the business and the uses to which the information will be put in analysis and planning; properly constructed, however, the funds flow statement accounts for all changes in the balance sheet and, properly interpreted, shows how funds were raised and spent. It is a better method than the balance sheet for showing, for example, trends in the use of trade credit, bank loans, accumulation of cash, stocks and so on. When viewed in perspective the various items may have more meaning; for example, a funds flow statement might show up the fact that increased bank borrowing had been used for reduction of creditors, or for an increase in credit extended to customers, or for an increase in stocks.

The flow of funds statement is useful therefore partly as a tool for the analysis of past financing and partly for future planning. It gives some indications of the results of current financial management, whilst not worrying too much about past events which have little influence on the future; it enables the manager to sort out the most significant changes which have taken place or are in process of taking place; it also shows in general the relationship between the various expenditures and the way in which they have been financed.

Since the major part of financial planning is based on cash flows, the flow of funds statement is a useful starting-point and a convenient historical reference for budgets.

The accounting records described in this section are drawn up in a form which enables them to be used for cash flow recording and planning; the balance sheet illustrated is fairly conventional apart from the fact that prior year data is omitted; the trading account, the income statement and the flow of funds statement are not in conventional form but in a form convenient for the identification of meaningful data and for the recording of cash flows rather than conventional book-keeping.

Financial and Operating Ratios

Historical accounting records may be put to other uses; one which may be particularly fruitful in certain circumstances is financial and operating ratio analysis.

Where such ratios can be meaningfully calculated, they have a number of uses: they can help in the evaluation of the financial position and performance of the business at any one time or over a period; they can assist in the planning and control of performance of costs; they can also be used as measures of efficiency.

But a cautionary note is needed: ratios are clues rather than conclusions; they reveal symptoms but do not provide cures or operating procedures.

The rationale of ratio analysis is simple; it is that any figure in a set of accounts has little meaning in isolation, and it acquires meaning only when it is seen in relation to other figures. A ratio is therefore a summarising figure, which has the advantage that it omits unnecessary detail and the corresponding disadvantage that some of the original information is lost or obscured.

When properly used therefore ratios are a convenient way of comparing information; when not properly used they can be misleading and can lead to wrong action. Many of the dangers may be avoided however by the simple device of refusing to see or evaluate any single ratio in isolation.

Three key ratios are normally distinguished:

(*a*) *Profit/capital employed* is conventionally used as a means of assessing efficiency in the use of business assets.

(*b*) *Profit/sales*, if read in conjunction with sales/capital employed, may help to explain variations in the ratio of profit to capital employed, and is useful as a guide in its own right to the profitability of the company's selling activities; normally the higher the ratio the better, but the actual level may depend on the business carried on (for example, a wholesaler might have a low ratio because his services and profit margin are a relatively small proportion of the final selling price, whereas a manufacturer at an early stage of production might be expected to have a fairly high ratio).

(*c*) *Sales/capital employed* shows how fully a business is employing its capital; normally the higher the better, but it may be too high if insufficient capital is employed.

There are serious measurement problems with all of the three key ratios; these are discussed shortly, but the main point at present is that neither capital employed nor profits are unambiguous terms.

Several other ratios may be calculated, for a whole variety of purposes. They fall into four main groups:

(*d*) *Liquidity ratios* are useful for showing the extent to which the company is maintaining a satisfactory level of liquidity, or ability to meet short-term debts. The two main ratios calculated under this heading are the ratio of current assets to current liabilities (*the current ratio*), which is a general measure of overall liquidity, but which includes in it some items which cannot be realised quickly in the event of need; second is the ratio of liquid assets (of which cash is likely to be the most important) to current liabilities less overdrafts, known as the *acid test ratio* because it shows the business's capacity to meet its liabilities quickly if the need arises.

(*e*) *Capital structure ratios* indicate the use to which various sources of funds are put; they show, for example, fixed assets, stocks, liquid assets, net worth, long-term debt, current liabilities, etc., as a percentage of total assets.

(*f*) *Secondary credit and performance ratios* include such items as stock to current assets, current liabilities to net worth, net worth to total assets, collection period of debts, creditors to debtors, stocks to sales, sales to fixed assets or current assets or stocks and so on; these may all be calculated for specific needs. There may also be a number of value added (or net output) ratios; profit to value added, for example, shows pretty clearly the profit on the activities which might be said to have given rise directly to such profits; value added to sales gives an indication of actual work done by the company; value added per employee is a fair productivity measure; value added compared with wages is another efficiency measure; in general, value added is a further explanatory measure which could be used much more widely than it is. Under this general heading one could also include various so-called *labour management ratios*, showing for example profit per employee, profit to wages and salaries and so on. It is also possible to calculate a number of *trend indices*, showing for example the trend of sales, profits or assets.

In *The Times* of November 29, 1968, the Editor of the Business News, Anthony Vice, outlined seven ratios set out by Mr. Arnold Weinstock of G.E.C., and recognised as his seven key criteria to assess acquisitions and to control the performance of divisions in his own group.

These are:

(1) profit on capital employed;
(2) profit on sales;
(3) sales as a multiple of capital employed;
(4) sales as a multiple of fixed assets;
(5) sales as a multiple of stocks;
(6) sales per employee;
(7) profits per employee.

Ratios may be used for two main purposes. First is as a straight check at any given time or over successive time periods of the business's own performance in isolation; second is as a basis of comparison with other concerns in the same field. The latter is perhaps more useful potentially, in that it gives the business a guide to where it stands competitively, but it does have several limitations. The Centre for Interfirm Comparisons, which is run by the British Institute of Management, operates a confidential service under which subscribers join a scheme for the comparison of key ratios of their own business with those of businesses which are roughly similar to themselves (see *Bib.* 49). Messrs. Dun and Bradstreet until recently also published lists of financial and operating ratios for a number of businesses in a wide range of industries (see *Bib.* 23); unfortunately publication of this valuable list has now ceased.

Some problems in the interpretation of accounting records*

Some of the problems of analysis of private company accounts arise from the different financial experiences of small and large companies: small private companies rarely make new issues of share capital or loan capital; they rely heavily on bank borrowing, trade credit and hire-purchase; they tend to have lower liquidity in general; they typically have higher levels of stocks and work in progress; and they tend to retain a higher proportion of pre-tax profits in the business. Any comparison between a private company and others must be interpreted with these differences in mind if misleading comparisons are not to be drawn. The financial pressures to which private companies are subject to some extent shape the ratios and determine their meaning and significance.

There are several problem areas in the analysis of the individual items of balance sheets and consequential difficulties in the interpretation of financial ratios calculated from them. If one wishes to compare two things uniform definitions are necessary; such uniformity is not easy to achieve. The three primary and explanatory ratios (profit to capital employed; profit to sales; sales to capital employed) require measurement of three items—assets, profits and sales—which provide cases in point.

Valuation is the main problem with assets. The main advantage of asset measures is that all companies are required to place a value on

---

* These notes lean heavily on *The Activities of Large and Small Companies* (see *Bib.* 14). I am grateful to the Editor of *Business Ratios* for permission to use the notes.

their assets at the end of the financial year. In practice the majority of companies start by basing their valuations on historical cost, revaluing from time to time as changes in price levels, etc., force them to realise that book values are not a true representation of the real value or earning capacity of the assets. But companies do not revalue simultaneously, and they do not revalue on the same basis; since most firms have complex asset mixes, with a spectrum of purchase dates, different lives, and subject to different price changes, it would be unreasonable to expect that all firms could readily put a realistic value on their fixed assets. The job for a large company is difficult enough, but many large companies can and do employ sophisticated techniques of valuation (although many of them still rely on old-fashioned preference for historical cost data); in small companies the task may be easier, because asset mixes may be less complex, but experience suggests that their techniques are pretty ineffective.

There is some evidence (see *Bib.* 12) that asset valuations in small companies tend to be too low; this is partly due to valuation techniques. In addition, since bigger and wealthier companies buy rather higher-priced, and frequently more efficient and productive assets, their asset figures will in any case tend to be proportionately higher than in small companies.

A further complication arises from the fact that balance sheets show the written-down value of fixed assets (and original cost of assets acquired since 1948). The Inland Revenue has strict regulations about the amounts which it will permit a firm to charge as depreciation (more strictly wear and tear) as a cost against tax; firms may, however, charge different amounts in practice but may not charge the whole amount against tax. The balance sheet value *should* represent the value net of actual (as opposed to Inland Revenue-permitted) depreciation; the investigator needs to make sure that it does, by checking with actual depreciation charged. The Companies Acts of 1948 and 1967 require the valuation and aggregate depreciation of fixed assets to be shown, and the user does have that information. There is no uniformity in methods of actual depreciation. Most economists would argue for some sort of replacement-cost basis in order to take account of changing price levels, but even this concept is not unambiguous since one needs to determine whether replacement cost is that of an identical asset, or a new model, or a second-hand alternative, or whatever. There is some evidence (see *Bib.* 12) that private companies typically charge depreciation at about 10 per cent. per annum on original cost: this looks suspiciously like straight-line depreciation for ten years.

Going-concern valuations of assets are rarely made; many accountants believe that there is no such thing, but this is part of what market valuations might be expected to indicate. Uncertainty about the basis of valuation of assets and the methods of depreciation used present problems for realistic analysis which cannot be ignored, for deviations do not tend to cancel each other out. Interpretation of the book value of assets of a company which has not recently re-valued its assets should certainly be cautious.

The valuation of stocks is another area in which practices vary considerably: normally the item on the balance sheet is "as valued by the managing director." It would be unlikely that the small firm would have such advanced methods of valuation as the large company, and such evidence as there is does suggest that historical cost is not infrequently used as a basis for valuing stocks in the small business. Larger firms may use LIFO (last in, first out) methods, which are fairly widely accepted nowadays by accountants for inventories; the use of FIFO (first in, first out) is, however, still fairly common.

Work-in-progress and finished-goods valuations depend to some extent on the costing practices employed by the enterprise. The large concern tends to use standard costing, marginal costing or other methods which enable the management to charge realistic prices for its products, although for internal costing and pricing purposes the products (and work in progress) may have nothing but notional or fictitious and unrealistic prices attached to them (this is a matter which has exercised progressive accountants but which, surprisingly, is ignored by a large number of concerns in practice). Small firms frequently have unsatisfactory costing systems.

The date of the balance sheet may also affect comparisons, since some companies deliberately choose a date when stocks are low. Although stock levels in small firms tend to be higher than in large concerns, their actual valuations may be proportionately lower and may thus contribute to the problem: methods of inventory control in small concerns are generally less efficient than in large.

The limitations of the sales figures are well known and the size of the entity depends, among other things, on the degree of vertical integration of the firm. Many small firms do little more than assembly jobs, and bought-out components are a high proportion of total costs; thus even within the same industry small concerns do different jobs from large ones and are frequently less capital-intensive (and therefore have lower overheads) with the result that turnover comparisons tell us very little. A turnover figure does not mean the same thing for all firms, and the interpretation of it and ratios based on it depends largely on a knowledge of the structure of the firm and the industry in which it operates.

There are many problems in using employment figures: the level of employment in a business depends largely on the nature of the concern, its capital intensity, its productive processes, the extent to which it employs part-time labour, the relative proportions of male and female labour, the ratio of operatives to other staff and the efficiency with which labour is employed. Thus any ratios (such as output per man, or capital per employee) cannot be interpreted in isolation and must be seen in the light of the other ratios and supplementary information. Small firms frequently have low capital productivity, but to take this fact at its face value (particularly for purposes of comparison) is unwise.

Profits are notoriously one of the trickiest areas of comparison. As a general rule in the examination of earning power, the more gross the measure the better (a consideration which is reinforced by the arbitrariness of most depreciation measures); net measures (net of depreciation, or tax, or dividends, or interest or any combination of these) may however be needed for certain purposes, such as policy decisions, and are of interest to shareholders and potential lenders in certain circumstances.

The profits of private companies tend to be smaller than those of public companies, and private companies tend to save more out of these smaller profits. These are useful and valid points to bring out in analysis, but they too are subject to qualifications which modify interpretations. Directors' remuneration is probably the key difficulty in the small firm, since directors' fees typically account for about 4 per cent. of total sales. In most small businesses the directors are also the managers, and directors' fees therefore contain a salary element; they also contain a dividend (or share of profit) element: Inland Revenue regulations allow directors' remuneration up to a point as a cost against tax. Thus directors' fees are partly salary and partly profit distribution: the former part should strictly be deducted from profit as a cost, the second should strictly be added back to profit. Inland Revenue regulations provide no guide as to how to allocate directors' fees and an attempt was made in *Determinants of Corporate Saving in Small Private Companies in Britain* (see *Bib.* 17) to make a realistic valuation: in 1956, out of an average directors' remuneration of £2,383 in a sample of private companies, the attributed salary element was £1,315.

The conventional accounting profit figure for a small company is therefore usually too low; if adjusted as suggested a rather higher profit figure emerges (and apparent losses of some private companies become profits). The same considerations apply to large companies, but in them the directors' remuneration figure is but a small proportion of total income and it has no real effect on profit figures. The general tendency in small companies to take some income and living expenses out of the firm, both as directors' fees and managerial salaries, means that profits are usually understated (a fact vehemently denied by many accountants).

Factually, profits of small private companies still turn out to be smaller on average than those of public companies; they pay smaller taxes, partly because of directors' fee allowances, partly because more of them make losses; they also pay smaller dividends (directors' fees play a part here too); at the same time they put a larger proportion of post-tax profits back into the business. An analysis of the ratio of non-quoted public company profits to assets (see *Bib.* 27) showed that they were on average higher than in quoted companies, partly because of low asset valuations in non-quoted companies, partly because many are subsidiaries of overseas companies which may in any case be more profitable (this is yet another example of the need to look behind ratios for explanation).

Moving away from the main ratios to other items, it is common practice to look at secondary performance and credit ratios involving current assets and liabilities of the concern. Current and liquid assets tend to be higher in small firms than in large concerns, and so do current liabilities. This is partly because of business needs and partly because of less efficient management of these items (both valid points for ratio comparisons); it is also partly due to the need for small concerns to use short and medium funds for capital purposes. Small growing firms depend heavily on creditors, and in their particular circumstances it is no use stating glibly that they are over-trading: they may well be, but to draw an invidious comparison between the small company and the large simply on a basis of balance-sheet figures of debtors and creditors or other current items is to miss the whole point. The comparisons do throw up important facts about the structure of financing of different sizes of business and about the problems of fund raising, but to use them as evidence of the credit-worthiness or performance potential of a firm fogs the issue and produces misleading answers.

Loans on the balance sheet also mean different things for different firms. Loans from directors and individuals rarely appear in the balance sheets of public companies, but they are relatively common in private companies; they are frequently key factors in their financing.

Loans from parent companies (many of which are overseas companies) should be treated differently from other loans since they are frequently of a capital nature in practice, even though they may be unsecured and the temptation may be to treat them as liabilities for purposes of analysis. The loan is a convenient way for a parent to finance a subsidiary and in some senses at least it is realistic to treat loans as equity; a quick and uninformed look at a ratio which includes such loans (say as liabilities) may give the wrong impression. It is also arguable that loans from such institutions as ICFC should be treated as equity rather than as liabilities. Similarly in businesses which are part of a group of companies, there may be a fairly large element of inter-company loans within the group; these may appear on the balance sheet and may yet again give a misleading impression. On the other hand, other financial help (such as cheap materials or components) may not appear on the accounts. Similarly, in some companies a certain proportion of bank loans should probably be treated as long-term debt (see later, p. 119).

Growth measures must also be interpreted in the light of these arguments. If conventions of measurement are kept constant part of the difficulty is removed and comparisons over time may be meaningful, but there may still be problems. The nature of the business may change for example. In addition, as is well known, a rapid growth in sales may be achieved at the expense of liquidity and over-trading, a growth in assets may be unprofitable and so on, and private companies are, on average, more liable than public companies to these dangers.

These points also have implications for flows-of-funds analyses. In the construction of such analyses there is the additional problem of making adjustments in order that book-keeping flows may be converted to real flows, *e.g.* by making allowance for bonus issues, revaluations, tax refunds, debts written off, etc. Some of these items are not always easy to identify from private company accounts and the item "other adjustments not specifically accounted for" may be proportionately large in statements for such companies.

In interpreting accounts it must be remembered that the balance sheet is merely a snapshot; it tells us what the books were like at the year end and nothing more. It may conceal more than it reveals (although practice in this respect has improved greatly), and other information is necessary if it is to be used properly.

Small companies will be unwise to measure themselves against public companies and against their industry in general: the whole basis of interfirm comparisons is the matching of like with like. Ratios themselves, helpful though they are, do not reveal all that is frequently read into them. It would be an imprudent businessman or lender who drew conclusions about a company from its ratios without trying to find out more about *its management and its potential.* These factors are always important; they are crucial when looking at the small company.

Conventional accounting records are honest recordings of historical events drawn up with a view to presenting an accurate picture of the stewardship of the company; rarely are they of much value for managerial decision-making or planning. But they can be reinterpreted in the ways outlined in this section; in the process they become much more useful.

BUDGETS

The accounting records discussed so far are historical and record the result of past operations. As such they are very useful, but if financial statements are to serve as instruments of planning and control they must also be drawn up for future periods, and must show cash flows.

Budgets are a means of formulating plans; they consist of series of projected financial accounts for future operating periods and show total expected expenditure, forecast value of sales and profits, and all cash flows and the timing of them. In a large company the budget needs to be set out in considerable detail, and each department has its own budget laying down what is expected from it in operating results. Such detail may be neither feasible nor necessary for many small businesses, but whatever the size of the business it must keep control of its cash position and at the very least a cash budget is an essential tool of small business planning.

In the course of its day-to-day activities the business needs to use cash to pay for materials, wages and overhead expenditures, and it will receive cash from customers; these will rarely balance from day to day or even from month to month, and the position is further complicated by the fact that many transactions are carried out on credit so that, even if the sales are made, the cash may not be coming in for some time. Thus extra cash may be needed to pay accounts before receipts start to flow in from activities which have to be paid for in advance. One of the commonest causes of financial embarrass- ment of the newly started business, and of the small concern which starts to grow rapidly, is a failure to take account of these elementary facts of business life; an astonishing number of growing small com- panies are highly profitable but insolvent. The cash budget enables the businessman to make advance provision, and there is nothing magical about it; it should enable him in particular to predict a cash deficit in advance and to make arrangements to cover it, and the arrangements will be a great deal easier if the deficit is predicted rather than if it is allowed to catch the businessman unawares.

For many small businesses a cash budget will be sufficient for much of the planning that will be needed; for more complex cases it may still be sufficient to prepare a sales budget, a stock budget, a creditors' budget and a debtors' budget, which will contain all of the key information.

A very simple example illustrates the principle. Mr. X sells sham- poos at £1 per bottle and pays the manufacturer 75p per bottle, giving him a profit of 25p per bottle of shampoo. At the beginning of the period he has been selling steadily at a rate of 1,000 bottles per month, but knows from his forecasts that he can now start to increase sales at the rate of 500 per month for a time; his supplier can supply him at this rate, but insists that Mr. X shall continue as he has in the past to pay him on the spot for the shampoos.

Table 13 shows how Mr. X will fare. He will sell as predicted, and by the end of month 4 will be selling at the rate of 2,500 bottles per month, bringing him a profit in month 4 of £625 and an accumulated profit over the four months of £1,750. But he has had to pay his supplier on the spot, and his costs have gone up from £750 in month 1 to £1,875 in month 4; at the same time he has not been able to collect his accounts receivable any more quickly, and his debtors have increased from a level of £1,000 in month 1 to £2,500 in month 4. Thus although he is making a healthy profit of 25 per cent. on turnover, he has run short of cash by the end of month 3 and has a cash deficit by the end of month 4.

TABLE 13

MR. X's BUDGET

Budget for:	Month 1	Month 2	Month 3	Month 4
TRADING ACCOUNT				
Sales	1,000	1,500	2,000	2,500
Less Costs	750	1,125	1,500	1,875
Profit	250	375	500	625
CASH				
Opening Cash	1,000	1,000	500	0
Plus Debts collected (previous month's sales)	1,000	1,000	1,500	2,000
Less Debts outstanding (current month's sales)	1,000	1,500	2,000	2,500
Closing cash	1,000	500	0	−500
DEBTORS				
Opening debtors	1,000	1,000	1,500	2,000
Less Sales in previous month (collected this month)	1,000	1,000	1,500	2,000
Plus Sales in current month (collected next month)	1,000	1,500	2,000	2,500
Closing debtors	1,000	1,500	2,000	2,500

By drawing up a budget he can predict this cash shortage, and, provided that he can convince the bank manager, he could probably get an overdraft to cover the deficit. What happens after the four-month period depends on whether he continues to expand or not; if he stabilises sales at 2,500 units per month the situation soon rights itself and his cash deficit will not increase; if he wishes to continue, a more permanent solution than bank borrowing is necessary.

In simple terms therefore Mr. X's business is profitable; his budgets show, however, that he will need some financial accommodation to maintain the cash flow necessary for the expansion of business.

A simple budget statement such as the example may be enough for many business operations; for the larger concern much more complexity may be needed, and the planning of operations may require a whole series of interlocking budgetary accounts portraying the future activities of the business as a series of financial accounts for future accounting periods.

Thus in the larger business each major department will have its own budget, laying down both in physical quantities and monetary terms what is expected from it in the budget period.

The main sectional budgets required in the more complex business are:

(a) *sales*, by product, by time period, possibly also by salesman, area, etc.;

(b) *marketing expenses*, appropriately subdivided;

(c) *production*, including plant utilisation, materials cost (preferably based on standard costing or the appropriate costing system of the organisation), labour cost (similarly determined), variable overheads budgets (covering indirect labour, factory supplies, lost time, repairs, maintenance, heat, light, power, inspection, storage, spoilage, etc.), fixed overheads budgets (covering costs of depreciation, supervision, rent, insurance, etc.) and a stock budget;

(d) *other departmental and sectional budgets* may include administration, promotion and advertising, cost of training, research and development, etc., depending on the nature and complexity of the business;

(e) *debtors' budget*, reflecting the customers' payment patterns, and based either on existing records or on proposed new methods;

(f) *creditors' budget*, reflecting the company's patterns of payment in the settlement of accounts with suppliers;

(g) *capital expenditure*, showing expected costs and forecast revenues on a cash flow basis;

(h) *master budget*, showing a *budgeted profit and loss account* (which should reconcile the sales budget with the various production, departmental and promotional budgets and should show the budgeted net profit) and the *budgeted balance sheet* (which should show the link between the opening actual balance sheet for the period and the budgeted balance sheet for the end of the period, which itself takes account of the operations of the business).

Budgetary planning is not as formidable as it might appear from such a list; the plans of the company usually bear some relation to what has gone before, and departments will be asked for their proposed future expenditure in relation to broadly determined objectives. Even so, there are perhaps two major lessons of budgetary planning: first is that the budgets are only as good as the forecasts on which they are based; second is that the budgets themselves may reveal areas in which improvement is necessary (a good example frequently found in practice is the identification of the need to collect debts more quickly; another common example is the revelation of the need for effective stock control).

Internal financial control

The discussion so far has concentrated on budgets as a planning device; their other main use is in control. The essence of budgetary control is that it provides a check on actual operations through the comparison of what has been achieved with what was intended. It is rarely to be expected that actual results will turn out to be the same as planned results. Deviations or variances may arise for a variety of reasons, through price changes, wage changes, changes in volume produced, changes in working conditions, changes in methods of production, overtime costs and so on. Not every departure from plan is necessarily bad, but it is desirable to have explanations for all deviations in order that action may be taken when necessary. But budgets cannot control everything, and it is necessary to treat them as servants rather than as masters of the operations of the business.

Flexible budgeting is designed to be responsive to changes which are outside the control of the business; markets, for example, may prove to be more buoyant than forecast, and it would not be sensible to refuse to meet the opportunities simply because the budget did not provide for an expansion. In the small business flexible budgeting is probably even more important than in the large one; small businesses cannot be expected to forecast as well as large ones, and in any case they are more likely to be affected by random chances, and the reasonable use of the budget in the small business is as a guide from which to depart if circumstances require rather than as a fixed plan.

In sum, budgeting and budgetary control in a small business can be relatively simple; it can rarely rise to very much detail; it must be treated as flexible; but it cannot be dodged, and in particular the difficulties of forecasting should not be used as an excuse for dodging the issue or for budgeting for too short a time period ahead (details may be different but time scales are the same for all sizes of business).

Other forms of internal financial control are also required. Even if cash budgeting is done properly, the cash which is available may be used wastefully in the form of excessive stocks, unduly long credit given to customers and so on.

One of the biggest problems in many small businesses is the excessively big or overvalued stock; the purpose of holding stocks of materials is nothing more than to bridge the interval between the availability of materials and an immediate requirement for them; stocks of finished goods are held in order to be able to meet the needs of customers on call; the average level of stocks needs to be related to the benefits derived from holding stocks balanced against the cost of holding them. The cost of holding stocks is frequently higher than is realised; it includes the interest charge on the money needed to finance them, warehousing costs, supervision costs and costs of obsolescence; on the other hand the cost of running out of stock may be the loss of an order, which may be too big for the small business to bear. It is possible to calculate economic order quantities by fairly simple methods, and more complex probability and queueing models may be developed for situations of great complexity or uncertainty; small businesses usually face more uncertainty than their larger brethren, and precise methods of stock control are not always profitable for them. A great deal of stock control can be done simply, by two-bin methods (useful if the value of the items is small but they are in frequent use), by regular checks on floor stocks and so on; similarly if the re-order time-lag is short, some risks can be taken. On the other hand, when stocks are expensive and represent a high proportion of the assets of a company, and when their carrying costs are high, and when "stock-out" costs are high, it will almost invariably pay to look at more elaborate methods for part at least of the stock; the increase in available cash alone may be worth the effort.

The other main area in which internal financial control may be satisfactorily employed is in the collection of debts. This is considered in more detail in a later chapter. It too can free cash and can result in the reduction of interest costs.

Value analysis, cost analysis, cost reduction and other managerial techniques may have similar effects, but they lie beyond the scope of this book.

Sound internal financial control can frequently ease the financial problems of the small business; it is perhaps unfortunate that many small businesses feel unable to afford the specialist advice which would enable them to set up such control, even though such advice usually yields more in returns than it costs. In extreme cases funds can frequently be raised internally by reorganisation without the need to look outside, and it is not uncommon to find in practice that many businesses which try to raise external funds prove on closer examination to be able to meet all or part of their immediate needs by such reorganisation.

Paradoxically, perhaps, some small businesses may pay too much attention to liquidity. The business needs to keep a certain level of liquid assets (normally cash) for meeting day-to-day needs, and funds surplus to these requirements may be invested in any of a number of ways; against these assets the business also has short-term liabilities, and it needs to keep a balance between the two. Conventional liquidity ratios, discussed earlier, are a guide to safety levels in this respect. But once a reasonable safety level has been achieved, excessive liquidity is little more than a fatty deposit on the business. Keeping money idle is inefficient; it is also inefficient to finance working capital entirely from short-term funds, because a great deal of working capital is in fact fairly long-term. It does not pay to exaggerate the importance of this point; excessive liquidity is inefficient, but excessive illiquidity is potentially suicidal. The only sensible answer lies in good cash-flow planning and budgeting, which shows when cash is needed and when it is not; provided that reasonable safety margins are kept it pays not to hold more cash than is necessary.

BREAK-EVEN ANALYSIS

A useful tool in the early stages of financial planning is break-even analysis, which in its simplest form identifies the point at which sales begin to produce profits, but which has more general uses in planning. Its essence is a recognition that all businesses have certain fixed costs at any given moment of time; these fixed costs must be met regardless of the level of output; there are also variable costs, which vary directly with output (there are also semi-variable costs, which fall between the two categories, but they need not concern us here since they merely complicate matters without adding anything to the explanation).

A simplified break even chart is shown as Figure 1, in which the company's fixed costs are £10,000, variable costs (mainly labour and materials) are incurred at the rate of £2,000 per thousand units of output, and expected sales revenue is at the rate of £4,000 per thousand units sold. The company breaks even at 5,000 units; below this level sales are less than costs and losses are made; beyond this level sales increase more rapidly than costs, bringing increasing profit per unit of output.

This is a very simple example. More realistic break-even charts would not portray either sales, costs or profits as single-valued or linear functions of output, but would show them as curves instead of straight lines; there would also be a recognition implicit in this that

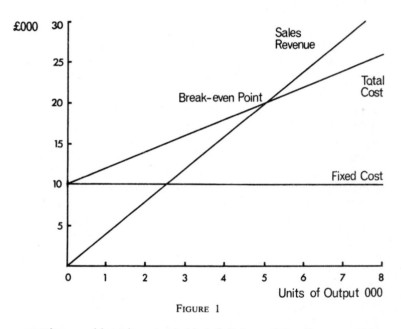

FIGURE 1

operations could not be extended indefinitely, and that there would be some limit on capacity beyond which there may be no profit; it would also be necessary to recognise that not all costs can be so conveniently divided into fixed and variable, and that in any case what is a fixed cost for the next twelve months may be variable in the longer run as it becomes possible to change plant and equipment.

But it is possible to take account of all of these refinements, and when they are admitted, break-even analysis has two main uses in financial planning.

First is in so-called marginal costing, where it found many of its earlier applications. The philosophy underlying this principle of costing is that fixed costs are unavoidable and that what matters is to cover variable costs and make some contribution to fixed costs; whether or not to accept an order or to make a product then depends on what contribution is made to fixed costs after variable costs have been covered. In the long run, of course, selling prices must cover fixed costs, and the success of a business which operated a marginal costing system would depend on maximising the total contribution; in circumstances where it was necessary to continue to supply special customers or to use some lines as attractions for others, marginal costing would not give the answer. But neither would any other system of costing, and indeed the use of break-even analysis as a costing tool is rather beyond the scope of the present book.

Its other main use is as a convenient device for exploring the implications of changes in the main elements of demand and costs. For example, a change in selling prices may be depicted as a change in the slope of the total revenue curve (a steeper curve showing a higher price and vice versa); a change in variable costs (as brought about by a change in overtime rates, material costs, changes in methods of production and so on) could be shown as changes in the slope of the variable cost line; the implications of changes in fixed costs, through capital expenditure, could be shown as different fixed cost lines and so on. This second main use is the main value of break-even analysis as a preliminary planning tool: it identifies the main areas of revenue and costs and enables the businessman to explore the possibilities; its main limitation is that it depends a great deal on the assumptions made and contributes little more than background information for cash-flow planning.

THE APPRAISAL OF CAPITAL EXPENDITURE

The decision to finance growth through large-scale capital expenditure is frequently one of the most difficult ones for the owner or manager of a business concern of any size; in small businesses this may be a make-or-break decision, and it is all the more important that it should be taken with full understanding of the implications.

Investment decisions are difficult because they take a long time to develop, and extend beyond the current accounting period, so that the results are not immediately apparent in the company's accounting records. Any capital expenditure also broadens the base on which profit is earned, which means that future capital expenditure must be at least as profitable as it has been in the past if earnings rates are to be maintained. The other main problem is that decisions which have implications which stretch far into the future also carry with them a great deal of risk and uncertainty, and the objective of good investment appraisal is to minimise the uncertainty and reduce the risk, although it is impossible to get rid of them altogether.

It is a truism that the basic investment decision merely asks the question: will the investment pay? More precisely, it asks whether adding to capital equipment now will increase the profits which can be earned sufficiently to justify the expense. The investment decision therefore has two parts, and is a balance between the costs and expected returns of the expenditure.

On the costs side there are three main elements. First is the capital cost of buying the equipment and ancillaries; second is the estimated addition to (or reduction in) operating costs; third is the cost of borrowing (or, as it is more frequently called in the literature, the cost of capital).

Capital and operating costs are usually not too difficult to estimate by competent surveyors, engineers, managers and other experts; the owner of a small business may face problems in this direction, but he should not be afraid to take expert opinion on this as on other aspects of the decision. One of the main problems with costs is that they tend to rise as time goes on, and in complicated decisions there is always the danger that something may be forgotten, or for tenders to be optimistic, or for some costs to be deliberately underestimated by those who want to have an idea accepted.

The costs of borrowing are an entirely different matter; they are the most difficult costs of all to estimate. Theoretical literature on the subject is wide, controversial and indecisive, and provides very little help to the businessman operating a small concern, about which just about the only sensible thing to say is that the cost of capital is high.

Perhaps the most important point of all, however, is that no capital is costless. Many small business proprietors are prone to think that, for example, retained profits do not have a cost of borrowing because they are already in the business and are, in a sense, a free resource; similarly, they may argue that accounts payable or income taxes payable are also free. This is an illusion; the real cost of such resources is what they *could* earn if they were put to some other use, such as the purchase of stock exchange securities, lending to local authorities, deposits with finance houses and so on; the economist calls these the opportunity costs, and they are very real in the sense that it does cost something to use any money at all, whether it belongs to the business, its proprietors or to outsiders.

Some other costs are just as real, but much less easily calculated; all of the sources of funds discussed later in this book have some disadvantages associated with them. New share capital, for example, carries a risk of loss of ownership, fixed interest capital carries a gearing problem, bank loans may be too short term and so on. If any of these things matter to the businessman, he must take them into account, and the disadvantages, or real costs, may be so high that he may have to decide against a particular piece of equipment or a particular growth plan.

The cost of capital from an outside backer is not easily calculated either. He may charge a fixed rate per year, which is simple enough. He may expect a given proportion of estimated total earnings, in which case the question is whether the *additional* earnings over and above those which would have accrued in the absence of the expenditure are greater than the price asked by the lender; if they are, the deal is a good one, if they are not, the expenditure should either be avoided or financed in another way. If the backer accepts equity, and is prepared to take whatever dividend on ordinary shares comes his way, the calculation is different again (indeed, it does not really have a precisely quantifiable answer).

Financial writers and advisers normally suggest that the cost of capital for a company should be a weighted average of all costs, which may be based on the price/earnings ratio of the company's share capital. Apart from the fact that few small companies have a price/earnings ratio, the calculations are usually beyond them in any case. If the outside backer is to be an institution such as ICFC, the backer will frequently be doing the calculations in any case, and will be looking at asset values, recent profits, price/earnings' ratios in similar businesses, the management and so on; part of the service of such institutions is that they will provide such advice.

But whether the company has such a backer or not, the final investment appraisal calculation requires a cost of capital against which to judge the expected returns, and the businessman must have a figure to put there. His calculation will take into account what he could get from lending his own money outside, what he would have to pay for fixed interest borrowing (which may range from bank overdraft rate to what he could expect to pay for a mortgage debenture); the figure which he comes up with will depend on how cautious he is, how much growth matters to him, and other imponderable factors.

None of which is very much help. In practical terms the answer probably comes down to two factors. First is that, even though retained earnings have an opportunity cost, their use in his own business is frequently going to give the businessman a better return than if he invested them outside the business. Second is that, with typical borrowing rates at the time of writing of over 10 per cent., the prudent businessman will be thinking of getting at least 15 per cent. and more likely 18 per cent. return on his capital. That is the sort of figure that he will be putting into his calculations as his cost of capital.

But it would be virtually impossible to defend these figures on theoretical or academic grounds.

On the returns side of the calculation there are two main needs: first is to make good estimates of the additional sales proceeds which the expenditure should generate; second is to employ soundly based yardsticks by which to judge the expenditure. The first is difficult; the second, although it employs what may appear to be difficult concepts, is much easier.

Estimation of future returns really requires some sort of forecasting procedure; but few small businesses can rise to this sort of thing themselves, and most are reluctant to employ outsiders for this purpose. The advice of writers and other pundits frequently consists of telling small businessmen to draw up long-range plans, or to adopt management by objectives, or whatever else happens to be fashionable; most of this sort of talk makes very little sense to the smaller businessman. But he does need to have some views of the future, and the decision to grow implies that he has some; he must also have a reasonably satisfactory past record of profits, and the management necessary to make the growth work. From this basis, he needs above everything else to be able to identify profitable opportunities for growth, to assess whether he can take advantage of them, given the strengths and weaknesses of his present organisation, to decide on what changes are needed (in markets, organisation and so on) and to make up his mind how much risk he is prepared to take. He must have some information about his markets, whether they are growing or declining, how many competitors there are, how they will compete, what causes changes in demand and so on; he should also have some view of the future course of events in the economy.

This reads rather like throwing in everything including the kitchen sink; so it is, but after all the major investment decision does cover just about every aspect of the business and cannot be seen in isolation; the bigger business may not need to go through the whole thing for each decision, because it has an overall strategy; for the smaller business the investment decision may be the whole of its overall strategy.

However good may be the tools of investment appraisal, they are only as good as the data which goes into the calculation; if the returns are badly estimated, discounted cash-flow calculations and the rest are not magic wands which will bring everything right in the end.

But the actual method of appraisal does affect the answer, and unsatisfactory methods may lead either to the acceptance of projects which lead to unduly low returns, or to the neglect of projects which may be potentially profitable.

There are three commonly used methods for the evaluation of capital expenditure; these are generally referred to as the payback method, the average rate of return method and discounted cash flow.

The payback method is the simplest, and one of the most commonly used; it merely indicates how long it will take to recover all of the money spent on a particular project. If for example a piece of equipment costs £10,000, and yields net profits of £1,500 per annum, plus depreciation at a rate of 10 per cent. per annum (£1,000) it will take four years to repay the original investment. The method has the advantage of stressing the fact that investment projects are not timeless, and timing of repayment enters into any calculation; it also emphasises that equipment can become obsolescent through time as well as wearing out through use. But it has disadvantages too: one problem is to choose an acceptable payback period (4–5 years is fairly common); it ignores profits which may come in later years (in fact it does not do so, but it pays little attention to them); emphasis on repayment perhaps places too much importance on liquidity at the expense of anything else; its result depends largely on the arbitrary choice of a rate of depreciation, and, most important, it takes no account of either the timing of cash flows or of the time value of money. The timing of cash flows is important; not all projects consist of one payment; neither do all cash inflows occur evenly over time; the time value of money is important for reasons to be discussed shortly. It is a cautious man's method, and it may lead to the neglect of profitable opportunities, but it is a good way of identifying obvious non-starters, and it works well for some businesses.

The average rate of return on investment may be calculated in a number of ways; the commonest method is to calculate net receipts (that is profit less tax and depreciation) and express them as a rate of return over the initial outlay for the number of years of life of the project; an alternative is to express the same amount of net receipts as a return on the average amount invested over the life of the project. This is a straightforward type of calculation, which may sensibly be used in the early stages of the evaluation of a project; it has the advantage over the payback method that it takes into account receipts over the whole economic life of the project. But it too fails to take into account the timing pattern of cash flows; it also uses arbitrary book depreciation figures; it looks at post-tax rates of return, which as will be seen, may be misleading; it, too, does not take into account the time value of money.

What is this time value of money about which so much fuss is made? It is essentially a very simple concept which has perhaps been dressed up to make it look rather too formidable. It is based on the recognition that a sum of money in one's pocket now is worth more than the same sum of money in a year's time, because during that year one could have invested that money at interest; it is also worth correspondingly more than the same sum several years ahead, because the interest could have been compounded. Thus future earnings of a capital project become less valuable the further ahead they accrue, and the earlier the profits come the more they can be reinvested to earn further income. In order to take account of this simple fact (which incidentally has nothing in itself to do with the fact that the value of money declines over time through inflation, although one can take that into account as well), future earnings are discounted back to the present. The process of discounting is nothing more than that of turning upside down the compound interest calculation and applying it to the net cash flows as they come in in successive years.

Discounting is, in other words, no more than deducting from future profits the rate of interest which they can earn by being put out at interest, thus showing profits over and above those which could have been made simply by lending the money to a financial institution. Or, looking at it the other way round, the discounted cash flow shows how much extra one has to earn in order to take account of the fact that money coming in next year is worth less than money in the pocket now.

Many businessmen feel that the time value of money is a lot of nonsense, and that in any case to the extent that it matters at all it is taken account of by the payback method, which sets a criterion under which the investment pays itself back quickly. But it can make a difference; for example if two projects yield similar sums in total (say £1,000) over three years, but one brings in £500 in the first year, £400 in the second, and £100 in the third, whilst the other brings in nothing in the first year, £100 in the next and £900 in the third year, the first project is preferable because by the end of two years £900 has come back in, and that can be reinvested to earn more money, whereas only £100 has come back to the second project.

But the method has other advantages too. Perhaps the most important of these is that it insists that all cash flows are shown net of all taxes and allowances, thus showing the net sum of money coming in from the project. This is important because the amount of tax paid does not depend on profits alone, but is effectively reduced by investment grants and annual allowances.

The processes of calculation for discounted cash-flow methods are fortunately not very complicated in principle, and are made much easier by the fact that tables of discount factors are widely published and may be used for discounting to give the present value of cash flows. But the calculations can get complicated in practice, particularly when cash flows start to come in at different times and so on. Calculations of this sort are perhaps best left to those with some experience of them; but they are not too difficult to learn.

Two main methods are used in practice. The *internal rate of return* method consists of identifying an interest rate (called the internal rate of return) which equates the present value of expected future receipts with the present value of the investment outlay; if the internal rate of return is greater than the cost of capital, the project is worth while. The *net present value* method identifies the present value of future receipts (cash flows) discounted at the company's cost of capital, minus the initial capital outlay; if the net present value is positive the project may be accepted.

In either case the simple rule is; the company should invest when the expected yield, suitably discounted, is greater than the cost of raising money. But the rule oversimplifies things too much because it does not take account of risk and uncertainty, which may be particularly large in a small business. One can gross up the discount factor by adding, say, another 7 or 8 per cent. for risk, and this is perhaps the simplest way; the alternative way, which requires estimates of the probabilities of various events and outcomes of courses of action, is really too complicated for the owners of small business.

Table 14 is a practical illustration of the working of discounted cash-flow calculations. It considers the case of a company which is deciding whether to buy a machine costing £50,000; the life of the machine is expected to be seven years, and at the end of that period the machine will have a scrap value of £2,000. Working capital requirements are £5,000, incurred at the beginning of the period. The forecast profits are shown in Column IV.

Column II shows the investment grant, which is paid to the company in the first year; in the example the grant is at 45 per cent. of the fixed capital outlay, this being the rate at which investment grants are paid in development areas.

Column V shows corporation tax, deducted in the example at the rate of 40 per cent. from the profits shown in Column IV; in practice, however, annual allowances against depreciation (at the rate of 20 per cent. of the initial fixed capital sum less the investment grant in the first year, and at 20 per cent. of the written down value from then on), and thus in Column VII the tax saving is calculated at the rate of 40 per cent. (corporation tax rate in the example) of the annual allowance.

In Column VIII the tax saving is deducted from the corporation tax payable in Column V, to show actual tax payable; it will be noted that in Year 1 the tax paid is negative, since corporation tax is not normally paid until after a delay of about one year.

Column IX shows the net cash flow after all of these adjustments; it consists of the sum of Columns II, III and IV, minus the amounts in Columns I and VIII (or, in the case of year, plus the tax refund of £2,200).

Column X shows the discount factors (which are simply looked up in a table of discount factors) for a rate of discount of 10 per cent.; these factors, which decrease each year and thus reflect the fact that the real value money in succeeding years goes down, are applied to the data in Column IX, and Column XI, which is simply Column IX multiplied by Column X, shows the net present

TABLE 14

DISCOUNTED CASH FLOW CALCULATIONS

Year	Capital Cost I	Investment Grant II	Scrap Value III	Profits IV	Corporation Tax at 40% V	Annual Allowances granted against previous year's profits VI	Tax Saved VII	Tax Payable VIII	Net Cash Flow IX	Discount Factor for 10% X	Present Value of Net Cash Flow XI
0	55,000	—	—	—	—	—	—	—	-55,000	1·0	-55,000
1	—	22,500	—	11,000	—	5,500	2,200	-2,200	35,700	0·91	32,487
2	—	—	—	12,000	4,400	4,400	1,760	2,640	9,360	0·83	7,768·8
3	—	—	—	16,000	4,800	3,520	1,408	3,392	12,608	0·75	9,456
4	—	—	—	16,000	6,400	2,816	1,126·4	5,273·6	10,726·4	0·68	7,294
5	—	—	—	15,000	6,400	2,253	901·2	5,498·8	9,501·2	0·62	5,890·7
6	—	—	—	12,000	6,000	1,802	720·8	5,279·2	6,720·8	0·56	3,763·6
7	—	—	2,000	10,000	4,800	1,442	576·8	4,223·2	7,776·8	0·51	3,966·2
8	—	—	—	—	4,000	3,767	1,506·8	2,493·2	-2,493·2	0·47	-1,171·8
											14,454·5

value of the net cash flow arising from the capital expenditure of £55,000.

At a rate of discount of 10 per cent., therefore, the net present value at the end of seven years of the investment project is £14,454·5. If the company's cost of capital is 10 per cent. therefore, the project is worth while, and using the net present value method gives this answer.

The internal rate of return may also be calculated from this table, but it requires the use of various discount factors, chosen by trial and error and experience, in Column X. Putting 20 per cent. as the discount factor in Column X, the net present value would be £1,173; putting 25 per cent. in as the discount factor would give a negative net present value (−£3,530); neither of these sets of calculations is shown in the example in detail. Interpolating between the two discount rates of 20 and 25 per cent. produces an internal rate of return of about 21·25 per cent.; since this is greater than the assumed cost of capital the project is worth while.

In practice the two methods can give different answers, but the reasons or details need not concern us here, and the principles illustrated in the example remain good: they are that the time value of money is an important determinant; that the cost of capital is a crucial element in the decision; and that capital grants and investment allowances make a very big difference to the outcome, underlining the importance of taking net-of-tax sums into account. The example also shows the importance of the first few years of working; the earnings profile (the technical term for the profits shown in Column IV) shows that earnings begin to tail off after Year 4, and the effect of this is enhanced by the fact that the discount factor decreases progressively.

There are other more sophisticated methods of investment appraisal, using linear programming, replacement theory, opportunity costs and other devices of operational research. They are unlikely to be of much interest to the owner of the small business. For him discounted cash-flow procedures are likely to be the most satisfactory, but he may well find it worth while to get the general dimensions of the problem from payback and rate of return methods first. In some small businesses, particularly in those which receive payment at the end of contracts, it may not be meaningful to talk of a cash flow at all (the jobbing contractor who takes on one biggish job at a time and gets paid when it is completed does not have a cash flow; he must, however, discount his final payment fairly heavily for the costs of borrowing and illiquidity which he has to bear in the meantime).

But none of the methods of investment appraisal are any good at all unless the businessman has gone fairly thoroughly into the prospects for his project; it is that analysis that matters, and the methods of calculation of rates of return are refinements which help him in the choice.

Summing Up

Several techniques and records may be employed in forecasting and in the preparation of plans to meet the cash requirements of the business: those discussed in this chapter include profit planning, accounting records, financial ratio analysis, budgets, budgetary control, internal financial control, break-even analysis and investment appraisal techniques.

The forecasting of cash inflows and outflows is the basis of all financial planning, and the timing of cash flows is as important as their magnitude.

Few of the techniques discussed in this chapter are very complicated in practice; the owner of the small business can learn to understand them fairly readily, even if he does not have the time or the inclination to do them himself. And the understanding of the uses of the techniques is more important than being able to do the calculations, for which experts can be engaged.

Detailed consideration of how to do the various calculations is beyond the scope and objectives of this book, which are merely to describe and outline the techniques and approaches.

CHAPTER 5

PROFITS AND INTERNAL FINANCE*

THE most important source of funds for the typical small firm is its own savings, derived from past profits.

There are two main functions of profit in the modern business enterprise: the payment of rewards in the form of dividends and other drawings to the owners and directors of the firm; and the provision of a source of funds, in the form of retained profits, for the maintenance and expansion of the business. The availability of this source of finance depends partly on the profitability of the firm, partly on the amount of tax which it has to pay and partly on policy with regard to distribution of profits.

PROFITABILITY

It may be expected, *a priori*, that small companies would be rather less efficient and profitable than large. It is not easy to compare performances in terms of profitability, but it is possible in rather a simple way to analyse certain components of manu-facturing costs, and to examine a few measures of profit and rates of return.

Broad categories of manufacturing costs are compared in Table 15. The data come from diverse sources, and are calculated in differ-ent ways. Oxford Survey data, for example, are presented in the form of both means and medians, the latter being necessary because the frequency distribution of firms in the sample is skewed, and the arithmetic mean gives a misleading impression (it may be swamped by a few large observations). The data in Column III (from the Census of Production) are calculated on a different basis: they in-clude some double counting of material costs due to interfirm pur-chases; material cost also includes transport (included in "other costs" in Oxford Survey data): value added excludes transport costs in Census data, and includes them in Oxford Survey data. The data in Column IV are calculations of macro-economic data from national

* References to the Bibliography are indicated, *e.g.* see *Bib*. 25; the Bibliography is to be found on pages 177–181.

income accounts, etc., and material costs exclude interfirm purchases.

When these reservations are taken into account, comparisons are tentative, but a reasonable interpretation is probably:

(*a*) material costs are relatively low in small firms;

(*b*) overhead costs and net output (value added) are therefore relatively high;

(*c*) there is also some evidence that wages and salaries tend to decline proportionately with size of firm (this is given a slight measure of support by Census data for 1954, which shows that in firms with 25–49 employees, wages and salaries were 20·6 per cent. of total sales. This declines to 18·0 per cent. for firms with 1,500–1,999 employees, but rises to 20·8 per cent. in firms with over 2,000 employees).

There is therefore some slight evidence of lower standards of performance in small manufacturing firms, and that labour costs are relatively high; this may be partly due to lower efficiency of labour in

TABLE 15

COSTS OF VARIOUS GROUPS OF FIRMS 1954

		Percentage of Total Sales			
		Small Firms [1]		*Larger Establishments* [2]	*All Manufacturing* [3] *Firms*
	Cost Item	I Median	II Mean	III Mean	IV Mean
I	Materials	45·0	44·1	56·1	45·8
II	Wages	28·6	34·1	19·6	35·4
III	Salaries	1·0	1·7		
IV	Depreciation	1·6	2·0	—	3·2
V	Other costs	11·9	12·4	—	—
VI	Total costs	94·5	92·6	—	85·1
VII	Sales	100·0	100·0	100·0	100·0
I & II & III	Direct costs	73·8	73·9	75·7	81·2
VII–I	Value added	56·0	54·1	43·9	54·2
VII–VI	Profit	7·2	8·0	—	14·9

Sources:
[1] Oxford Survey. Neither median nor mean add up to 100 per cent. Both medians and means are calculated from grouped frequency distributions.
[2] Calculated from data in *Census of Production of the United Kingdom,* 1958.
[3] E. T. Nevin, "The Cost Structure of British Manufacturing," *Economic Journal,* Vol. 123, pp. 642–664.

small firms, which may itself be partly a reflection of low capital intensity. The evidence in Table 2 lends some support to these observations, in that it shows that both net output per head and capital expenditure per head tend to decline as the size of the enterprise shrinks, but too much reliance cannot be placed on the comparisons. Inter-industry differences are frequently considerable, and these may well cut across size classifications. (For a fuller discussion of some of the limitations of these comparisons see *Bib.* 12.)

The measurement of profitability presents even greater problems. Two types of ratio are frequently calculated: one expresses a profit measure (however defined) as a return on sales, the other as a return on assets or capital employed. The nature and problems of such ratios are discussed on pages 48–54.

Profit on sales can be a dubious concept, since the sales figure may depend heavily on material costs (for example, the sales or turnover figures of wholesalers are high because they spend a lot on stocks and add little value to them, sales figures of any enterprise at the end of a long chain of productive activities would be similarly high, whereas in proportion the sales of a coal-mine would be relatively low because material costs are low, whilst wages and value added are extremely high). Between similar firms in the same industry profit/sales ratios may yield meaningful comparisons; between diverse enterprises the comparisons would mean little.

Profit on assets or capital employed may seem to be a simple enough measure, but it too presents many problems in the choice and valuation of the assets concerned.

Profit measures themselves also cause a great deal of difficulty in practice. It may be argued that the net-of-tax return to shareholders is the appropriate measure of profit, since it is this sum which influences policy decisions and is of crucial interest to shareholders and potential new investors. Since tax rates fluctuate, and may also be subject to rebates, allowances, etc., it is also arguable that the sum left at the disposal of the company is the only figure which has any meaning over any long period of time.

At the other extreme, however, it is arguable that what the economists should really attempt to measure is the earning capacity of the enterprise, and that this is best expressed by using the grossest possible measure of profit. What happens to this gross income is arguably a separate issue. The case for this view is strengthened when the investigator is employing published accounts for his data, since depreciation allowances are pretty arbitrary, and a measure which does not depend on such allowances is normally preferable.

Gross Profit (defined simply as sales minus total costs) on turnover of small firms in manufacturing is lower (between 7 and 8 per cent.) than that of all manufacturing firms (14·9 per cent.) (see Table 16), even though value added (or net output) is similar in the two groups at between 54 and 56 per cent. Both of these comparisons show profit net of depreciation, which is 1·6 per cent. (median) in small firms, and 3·2 per cent. (mean) in all firms; adding back depreciation widens the gap. This is a crude comparison, but it is probably worth making.

The median ratio of turnover to net assets in private companies in 1954 was 3·4; this compares with an average of 2·2 per cent. for all United Kingdom companies between 1957 and 1964. The difference is probably due to poor techniques of asset valuation in private companies.

Two measures of profit on net assets are shown in Table 16. The arithmetic mean for Oxford Survey firms is lower than that of quoted public companies, but the median for Oxford Survey firms is higher for both measures. It is unlikely that this means that small private companies are more profitable than public companies; it is much more likely that asset valuations are too low in small concerns. The net of tax return of private companies may be proportionately high because of the relatively low tax payments of these firms.

TABLE 16

PROFIT/NET ASSET RATIOS OF PRIVATE COMPANIES
AND QUOTED PUBLIC COMPANIES 1956

	Gross Profit/Net Assets	Net Profit/Net Assets
Private companies (median)	18·2	10·5
Private companies (mean)	11·9	5·9
Public companies	14·5	8·7

Gross profit is defined as trading profit (total sales minus total costs), minus depreciation, plus other income (depreciation accounted for about 20 per cent. of gross profit in both private and public companies). Net profit is defined as gross profit minus tax. Net assets are defined as total assets minus accumulated depreciation minus current liabilities.

Sources: Oxford Survey and *Bib.* 82.

It is also interesting that, as shown in Table 17, the ratio of net profit to net assets of non-quoted public companies was higher during the period 1960–1962 than the same ratio for quoted public companies. An analysis of this data in *Economic Trends* (see *Bib.* 27) advanced possible explanations: first was that non-quoted companies may have less efficiently calculated and lower assets valuations (a similar reason to that given above for private companies); second was that many of the non-quoted companies are subsidiaries of overseas companies, which may be more profitable, possibly because of better "know-how", possibly because of better management, possibly because the overseas company may restrict its United Kingdom marketing to goods of proven quality. The article in *Economic Trends* also demonstrated that in trades in which overseas parent companies are less important, the earnings/assets ratios of quoted companies are higher than those of non-quoted companies.

TABLE 17

INCOME NET OF TAX AS PERCENTAGE OF NET ASSETS

	Non-quoted Companies	Quoted Companies
1960	22·9	16·0
1961	20·2	13·8
1962	17·3	12·5

Source: *Economic Trends*, February 1965, Table F, p. ix.

Too much reliance should not therefore be placed on the comparisons of Table 16. Median net profits/net assets of around 10 per cent. for private companies and an arithmetic mean of 5·9 per cent. compare with an average for quoted public companies for the period 1950–1964 of 8·7 per cent. Returns on equity capital (net assets minus preference shares and minority interests) in quoted public companies ranged between 7·7 and 11·7 per cent. between 1949 and 1965 (11·2 in 1954) (see *Bib.* 62); since few private companies have either preference shares or minority interests, this may be a more realistic comparison, which reduces even further the comparative profitability of smaller concerns.

J. F. Boswell (see *Bib.* 21) found that there was some evidence that firms financed by ICFC were rather more profitable than quoted companies. He interpreted this fact with reservations; it is worth noting, however, in the first place that ICFC know how to select good companies and would be expected to choose those which are better than average, and secondly, that the very fact of being backed by ICFC would help a business to become more profitable.

These tentative comparisons suggest that:

(a) profit on turnover of private companies is lower than that of public companies;

(b) there is not much difference between the two groups in terms of income/asset ratios, but given that asset valuations are suspect in small concerns, it is likely that private companies are relatively less profitable than public companies in these terms also.

THE DISPOSAL OF INCOME

Small and large concerns also differ when it comes to the distribution of profit.

Table 18 compares two samples—of private companies and quoted public companies—and shows up some interesting differences. Tax payments are relatively small in private companies; private companies pay very small dividends (the mean figure for private companies is inflated by a small number of large payments by bigger companies in the sample); private companies also tend to retain a higher proportion of total profit than public companies, probably retaining more out of proportionately smaller total earnings.

TABLE 18

THE APPROPRIATION OF INCOME 1956

	Percentages of Total Profit			
	Private Companies		Quoted Public Companies	
	Median	Mean	Median	Mean
Tax	33·7	28·2	56·1	56·5
Dividends	—	15·9	17·8	18·8
Retained profit	54·8	59·6	44·5	46·7

Sources: See *Bib.* 12.

Tax legislation at the time of the Oxford Survey and that current at the time of writing both favour profit retention as against distribution.

Close company rules actually work the other way in that they require such companies to distribute a high proportion of profits. The legislation for close companies is complex, but in its simplest terms it means that if the company makes profits it can claim ordinary depreciation allowance; it can also claim directors' fees as an allowance against tax (although there may be complications in some cases) and there are other small allowances. The company then pays corporation tax in the normal way, at whatever is the going rate; dividends are subject to personal taxes on their recipients. Unless the close company distributes 60 per cent. of trading profits (and the whole of distributable investment income) however, the Inland Revenue may make a "shortfall assessment," and levy tax as if such dividends had been paid; exceptions are allowed if the company can show a need to retain profits for business reasons.

Private companies do not therefore have a lighter real tax burden, nor do they find financial circumstances easier because they retain a higher proportion of their profits. The absolute levels of both profit and tax are low in such companies and there is a scale effect because of this, since levels of retained profit may be inadequate for self-financing even at low levels of activity.

Dividends are low in private companies: the median is zero (*i.e.* over half of the firms in the Oxford Survey paid no dividends at all); quoted public companies, on the other hand, paid relatively high dividends. Dividend policy is complex: it is affected partly by taxation, but in quoted public companies the need to raise outside capital on the New Issue Market has a significant influence in that adequate past dividend levels are one of the factors affecting the likely success of a new issue. This consideration applies to private companies only at certain stages of their career (notably when they are considering whether or not to become public companies); thus they need to pay less attention to dividends and can pay out a higher proportion of their profits as directors' fees.

The only other thing that companies can do with their net-of-tax profit is to retain it in the company, although what they do with the funds afterwards offers plenty of alternatives.

It has long been a matter of argument whether companies decide on profit distribution with respect to dividends or to retained profits. There is evidence (see *Bib.* 17) that many companies first decide on a dividend level, and do so by asking whether to change the existing dividend level, and if so by how much; savings in such cases are a residual. Other companies decide first on the amount which they wish to retain in the business for safety, expansion and so on. The final decision is a balance of the two, but companies differ in their priorities, and there appears to be no general rule.

Part of the explanation of the relatively low tax and dividend items in private companies lies in the way in which directors are paid. The majority of firms in the Oxford Survey were family owned and director-controlled and when faced with a choice of whether to pay directors via fees or dividends, normally chose the former. Directors' remuneration is an important cost item in most private companies, typically accounting for about 4 per cent. of total sales. The Inland Revenue authorities are prepared to allow directors' remuneration as a cost to the firm within certain limits; it is therefore advantageous to the firm to pay directors' fees rather than dividends (which do not count as costs), it is also better for the individual to receive a fee, which ranks as earned income for tax purposes, rather than a dividend, which is unearned income.

It is possible therefore to treat directors' fees either as distribution of income or as a salary item (representing a managerial wage), but to treat fees as exclusively one or the other would be to overstate true income (in the first case) or to understate it (in the case of a salary item). The upper limit on allowable fees is so low that in large firms the dimensions of the problem are small enough to permit it to be ignored; in private companies in the Oxford Survey, however, the effect was considerable. In 11·5 per cent. of firms, what appeared to be losses became profit if earnings were expressed gross of directors' fees, and in general treatment of fees as a cost tends to understate real profits considerably.

An estimate has been made (see *Bib.* 7) of the salary element of directors' remuneration (*i.e.* that part of remuneration which might be looked on as a managerial wage rather than as a distribution of profit): this was £1,315 p.a. in Oxford Survey firms in 1956, out of an average total directors' remuneration of £5,383, and out of a profit net of directors' remuneration and gross of depreciation of £6,926. This means that a truer statement of gross profit would be £6,926 + (£2,383 − £1,315) = £7,994. Dividends were £833 on average; adding back the dividend element of fees this became £833 + (£2,383 − £1,315) = £1,901. Neither median nor mean profits or dividends in Table 18 have been recalculated to allow for these adjustments, but an approximate weighted arithmetic mean of restated dividends as a percentage of restated profits is 24 per cent. Small firms therefore appear to pay proportionately smaller tax than quoted public companies, partly because of the statistical effects of directors' remuneration, and partly because on the whole a larger proportion of private companies make losses (17 per cent. of the Oxford Survey sample made losses in 1954, 21 per cent. in 1955 and 17 per cent. in 1956).

The 1965 Finance Act introduced limits on the amounts of directors' remuneration allowable against tax, and the legislation was rather severe on close companies; the restrictions were removed in the 1969 Finance Act.

S. J. Prais points out (see *Bib.* 82) that the circumstances of the shareholders of very large firms vary considerably—some may rely, as do insurance companies, on dividend income, whilst others may wish the company to save in what they conceive to be everyone's long-term interest. This distinction may also apply to shareholders of small concerns: few insurance companies invest much in small firms, but many small shareholders may depend on their dividends for income (their influence would depend on their voting power and influence with directors). Prais also points out that as larger companies must exhaust possibilities for profitable expansion, in time their controllers will accept higher taxation on dividends in order to be able to invest in other concerns: here the directors of the small firm are favoured since they can pay themselves fees at lower tax rates. Similarly, the desire to avoid take-over bids may cause companies to try to keep their dividends fairly close to the general average for the same type of concern.

In the short term other factors may influence distribution policy. Larger concerns (particularly the giant public companies) may expect their incomes to remain fairly stable over a long period whilst fluctuating considerably in the short run: they would be unlikely to let a short-term variation in profits affect dividends; and dividends may therefore be a fluctuating proportion of disposable income. They also try to avoid ever having to reduce their dividends. Other firms may feel less confident of their long-term stability in terms of profits and one would expect that the dividends of these firms would show a closer relationship over time with disposable income; but even these firms might be expected to have reserves adequate for one year's fall in profits and there may well be some time-lag before dividends adjust to income.

But dividends are so small in most small businesses, shareholders are so few, and directors are of such importance that these factors probably had little influence when compared with the predominant importance of directors' remuneration.

Whatever their policy, retained profit is higher as a proportion of both gross and net profit in private than in quoted public companies, the former retaining typically about 55 per cent. in 1956 compared with about 46 per cent. in the latter group. This does not mean that small companies are thriftier than large, since they are merely retaining a larger part of a proportionately smaller income. Comparisons have been made (see *Bib.* 17) of the marginal propensity to save (the proportion of an increase in gross income which a company retains) of various groups of companies.

A least-squares cross-section regression of saving on profit for a sample of eighty-one firms in the Oxford Survey gave:

$$R/A_t = -0.07 + 0.79\ P/A$$
$$(0.02)\ \ (0.03)$$

where R is retained profit or saving, A is net assets, P is profit before tax and depreciation and adjusted in the light of the salary-dividend consideration mentioned earlier ($r^2 = 0.88$). Figures in parenthesis denote standard errors. The implication of this equation is that a unit increase in the rate of profit on net assets led to a 0.79 unit increase in the rate of saving on net assets. This is slightly lower than the marginal propensity to save of a sample of quoted public companies in the United Kingdom (0.73) but the difference is not statistically significant at the 5 per cent. level. The two sets of results are brought even closer together if consideration is given to the effect of dividends in the previous year (on the grounds that firms pay attention to maintaining some sort of consistency in dividend payments). This hypothesis gave:

$$R/A = -0.0129 + 0.86\ P/A - 0.59\ D - 1/A$$
$$(0.02)\ \ \ \ \ \ \ \ \ (0.06)$$

where $D-1$ is the previous year's dividend ($r^2 = 0.95$). The marginal propensity to save (with lag) is therefore 0.86; lagged dividends have a negative effect (*i.e.* the higher last year's dividend, the greater the pressure this year for dividends at the expense of savings). This compared with a marginal propensity to save of 0.85 in the sample of quoted public companies, and a coefficient for lagged dividends of -0.66 ($r^2 = 0.98$).

This suggests that, contrary to expectation, small firms do not save a larger proportion of an increase in profit than large firms (although the averages, as shown by Table 18, may differ).

Unquoted public companies may be expected to behave differently from both private and quoted public companies, since they come somewhere between the two (they are usually bigger than private companies but smaller than quoted companies, and they do not have such good access to sources of funds as quoted companies but are better off in this respect than private companies). A comparison of the appropriation accounts of companies in the three categories appears in Table 19. Weighted arithmetic means are used in this table.

TABLE 19

PERCENTAGE APPROPRIATION OF GROSS INCOME OF PRIVATE, UNQUOTED AND QUOTED PUBLIC COMPANIES, UNITED KINGDOM 1956 AND 1962

	I	II	III
Depreciation	17·2	21·5	14·8
Tax[a]	29·3	37·5	33·7
Interest on long-term loans	—	1·9	3·1
Minority interests	—	0·7	1·1
Dividends[b]	23·8	20·9	18·5
Retained income	29·7	17·5	19·8
Gross income[c]	100·0	100·0	100·0
Total gross income	£7,994	£492,905	£1,136,227
Number of companies	144	468	2,200

NOTES

I Small private companies.

   Source: Oxford Survey data for 1956. Directors' remuneration has been split into two components, the salary element being deducted from gross income as a cost and the dividend element being added back to dividends.

II Unquoted public companies, 1962.

   Source: "Non-quoted Companies and their finance," *Economic Trends*, February 1965.

III Quoted public companies, 1962.

   Source: as II.

[a] Tax includes prior year tax adjustments.

[b] Dividends are shown net of tax.

[c] Total Gross Income is defined as Trading Profit plus other income (from investments, etc.) plus prior year adjustments other than tax.

   Where column totals do not exactly equal the sum of elements this is due to rounding.

Part of the differences between the groups of companies is due to their different financial circumstances and requirements, which are discussed later; others may be briefly commented on, and used as a summary:

(a) Small firms on average save more from their income than do larger ones, the marginal propensity to save is however not significantly different between small and large concerns.

(b) Small firms pay negligible long-term interest and have

negligible minority interests: the former characteristic is probably due to the fact that, because they are risky and unattractive prospects, small firms can rarely obtain long-term loans, the latter to the fact that they are usually too small to have subsidiaries. On the other hand, bank and other short-term loans, which are widely used, are at fixed rates of interest and may be very important in many small businesses.

(c) The lower tax of small firms is partly due to the directors' remuneration element, and partly due to the fact that smaller firms are more likely to make losses.

(d) Small firms are subject to two opposing pressures when deciding on dividends: the first is the need to save for expansion, the second represents the tax advantages of distributing profits in the form of directors' remuneration. When account is taken of the second of these pressures, small firms probably pay similar effective dividends to large concerns, but do so via directors' fees. Small firms perhaps need to pay less attention than quoted companies to the need to keep shareholders relatively happy in case of new capital issues.

(e) The larger average savings of small firms result more from necessity than from financial ease, since they have to make larger provision for self-financing; similar marginal savings suggest, however, that they do not increase the rate of saving as profits grow.

(f) The saving and dividend behaviour of unquoted companies is nearer to that of quoted companies than private companies; there are slight differences in most items, but it is very doubtful whether they are statistically significant.

OTHER INTERNAL SOURCES

The firm has other internal sources: the most important is depreciation; and in addition future tax reserves and liquid assets may both be used to provide finance.

Depreciation

Wear-and-tear allowances permitted by the Inland Revenue are allowed as costs against income but, being computed on a historical cost basis, they rarely represent true depreciation of assets. Methods of depreciation vary from business to business; they are briefly discussed on page 49–50. Firms which only put aside the permitted sums for depreciation are in fact failing to make provision for keeping the capital value of their assets intact: many firms do put aside more than the amount allowed by the Inland Revenue, but they are not allowed to escape tax on these sums. Depreciation allowances are a significant source of gross saving in small firms.

There is a reasonably clear theoretical economic criterion of retained profit: any income transferred to reserves over and above what is necessary for the maintenance intact of the net worth or earning capacity of the enterprise is retained profit; strictly, therefore, depreciation provisions are not part of retained profit but are part of the funds necessary for maintaining earning capacity, but in practice there are so many problems with the valuation of assets and depreciation practices that a distinction is not always practically possible and it is frequently convenient, though theoretically indefensible, to consider all undistributed income as one flow of funds from which the firm will replace its assets and undertake any expansion. The case for this is strengthened when it is considered that many firms, when buying plant, etc., are in fact doing two things— replacing old assets and buying new ones—and the distinction between the two is rarely clear when technical obsolescence makes comparison of old and new meaningless.

Future tax reserves

Although future tax reserves are a committed liability, and have to be used eventually to pay the Inland Revenue authorities, in the short run they can be used by the firm as a source of funds. Additions to these reserves are much the same in principle as additions to other reserves and are simply allocations from the profit and loss account. Additions to future tax reserves arise because a firm has to pay tax in each year on the basis of earnings in a previous year; and a company whose income (and hence its tax liability) is rising has to put away increasing sums to future tax reserves. Companies with falling income make annual subtractions from future tax reserves on the balance sheet; these are thus a use of funds.

In very few cases are future tax reserves a significant item in the balance sheet of small businesses; some firms with no future tax reserves at all make zero, negative or very small profits, and consequently have no need to put by sums for tax payments in the future. But some firms in this category earn relatively high taxable profits: they either rely on meeting future tax liabilities out of income earned in the year when payment was due, or fail to make provision. It is not uncommon for the small firm to fail to make provision in this way, frequently with unhappy consequences.

Liquid assets

The firm has one other possible internal source of funds: its liquid assets in the form of marketable securities, tax reserve certificates and cash. Normally the firm keeps a certain level of liquid assets (usually cash) for meeting day-to-day liabilities; and funds surplus to these immediate requirements (but which may be needed in the long run) are invested in marketable securities of one kind or another where they can earn an income and not be completely idle until needed.

Against these liquid assets the firm also has short-term liabilities, and in certain senses it is more realistic to consider the liquid position of the firm as net of such liabilities. The principal liability of this sort is bank credit, but the firm also has two other liabilities which it has to meet in the very short term: dividends and current tax.

TABLE 20

NET LIQUID POSITIONS OF PRIVATE, UNQUOTED AND
QUOTED PUBLIC COMPANIES 1956 AND 1962

	Percentage of total number of firms			
	I	II	III	IV
Net liquid assets as percentage of net assets:				
Minus 10 and over	48·6	23·1	—	—
0–9.9	10·0	14·8	—	—
Plus 0–9.9	10·0	18·0	—	—
10 and over	31·4	44·1	—	—
Average	—	—	−6·6	−4·6
Median	−6·4	+6·6	—	—

NOTES:
I Private companies 1956.
II Quoted public companies 1956.
III Unquoted public companies 1962.
IV Quoted public companies 1962.
Sources: Oxford Survey, and *Economic Trends*, February 1965.

The net liquidity of a business may therefore be seen as a balance between its liquid assets and its short term liabilities; in Table 20 net liquid assets are shown as a percentage of net assets: in 1956 private companies typically had negative net liquid assets, but experience varied a great deal from firm to firm; quoted public companies in

1956 had positive net liquid assets; in 1962, however, both quoted and unquoted public companies were illiquid in the sense that they had short-term liabilities in excess of liquid resources. It is worth adding, however, that, since quoted public companies tend to extend more net trade credit than unquoted public and private companies, they are probably rather more liquid in the long run. This may well help to account for some of the other observable differences in financial behaviour of small and big business.

Other ways of measuring liquidity are shown in the brief discussion of financial ratios on pages 45–54.

Changes in the net liquid position of firms represent sources of uses of funds: an increase in the net liquid assets being a use of funds, a decrease being an increase in debts, or a source of funds.

There is a tendency for growing small firms to make rather more use of liquid assets as a source of funds than for other businesses to do so.

But it is necessary to keep a sense of balance about liquidity. Some liquidity is essential; too much is a waste of resources because it ties up working capital in a use which produces no return. This point is discussed in further detail in Chapter 4.

SELF-FINANCING

Small firms rely more heavily than large on their own savings for expansion, and Prais has shown (see *Bib.* 82) that the very biggest public companies also tend to plough back slightly more of their profits than do other public companies. In almost three-quarters of firms in the Oxford Survey retained profits were over 5 per cent. of net assets (the median in 1956 was 9·2 per cent.), whereas the average for all but the very fastest-growing public companies is under 5 per cent.; even given the undervaluation of assets in private companies, the differences are probably important. The data in Column I of Table 7 in Chapter 1 may slightly exaggerate the importance of retained profit as a source of funds. Non-quoted and quoted public companies tend to retain similar profits as a proportion of total funds.

The degree of self-financing may be measured in other ways. Two possible ratios are:

(i) a ratio of gross company savings (retained profits plus depreciation plus prior year adjustments) to material investment in fixed assets (also gross of depreciation) and stocks;

(ii) a ratio of gross company savings (defined as in (i) above) to expenditure on operating assets (fixed assets gross of depreciation plus stocks plus changes in net trade credit granted or received), or what might be considered expenditure on fixed assets and working capital.

These two ratios are shown in Table 21 for three groups of companies. Unfortunately for the purposes of this comparison, investment expenditure tends to be undertaken at longer intervals than one year and in fairly large discrete quantities, whilst saving is

TABLE 21

THE RELATION OF SAVINGS TO EXPENDITURE

	Savings/ Investment	Savings/ Expenditure on Operating Assets
I *Private Companies* 1954		
Median	55·0	39·2
Mean	204·7	123·1
II *Quoted Public Companies* 1954		
Median	135·7	53·1
Mean	133·9	54·1
III *Non-quoted Public Companies* 1960–62		
Mean	64·2	79·3
IV *Quoted Public Companies* 1960–62		
Mean	70·0	67·7

Source: See *Bibs.* 12 and 27.

more continuous; this means that year-to-year data may not reflect typical long-term experience. The typical ratio of savings to investment in private companies between 1954 and 1956 was between 55 and 65 per cent., but fluctuations over time were large, and differences between firms were considerable; in large public companies the ratio was 136 per cent. (this may not be typical of all quoted public companies, however, since Tew (*Bib.* 82) found that on average during 1949–1953, their self-financing ratio was 86 per cent.). The averages for non-quoted and quoted public companies were down to 64 and 70 per cent. respectively in 1960–1962. There is some internal evidence, discussed in the first edition, that the data for small private companies may not be entirely typical: for example, the figure for investment was understated in some firms by large stock reductions; in many companies on the other hand investment was negative. More detailed analyses of the private company sample suggest that the slower-growing, highly liquid firms in the sample were more likely than the sample as a whole to be self-financed, and it is possible that a high degree of self-financing indicates a cautious and slowly developing enterprise.

The financing of expenditure on operating capital follows a similar pattern: the degree of self-financing in private companies is lower than in quoted public companies; in unquoted public companies the relatively high ratio of savings to expenditure is partly due to a high level of net trade credit received, which proportionately reduced the size of expenditure.

There is more of a tendency to self-financing in private companies than in public companies.

COMPANY SAVING AND THE FINANCING OF SMALL BUSINESS

Internal finance has always been one of the most important sources of funds for business enterprise, and it will remain so. Many of the giant firms which we know today grew during the nineteenth century by ploughing back profits into the business; and indeed until after the First World War it was rare for any business to raise much of its long-term capital outside the firm, very few companies had shares quoted on the Stock Exchange and even fewer made public issues of shares. In the last fifty years increasing taxation has made it more difficult for companies to plough back profits adequate for expansion, and the capital market has devoted more of its attention to the financing of industrial companies, with the result that the bigger concerns are tending to raise a higher proportion of their funds outside the firm.

Even so, quoted public companies rely on internal finance for about two-thirds of all of their funds and internal finance is still the most important source of funds for big business.

This is even more true of the small firm. When an individual sets up in business (and he will frequently do so on his own account or with a partner) his own capital is likely to be the main source of his funds. He may have saved it, or had a windfall in the shape of a legacy or some other gain; but without his own capital he is unlikely to be able to set up. He may receive help from others, but only if he is able to impress relatives, friends or acquaintances that he is a fit person to whom to lend for business purposes; and in most cases it is an individual's own capital which provides a start for the business.

As time goes on he will receive credit from suppliers and from the bank, and perhaps even from customers; and he may be able to buy plant on credit or lease it. But if the business prospers he will frequently wish to extend further. Profits will have grown, but the businessman may have a difficult job deciding what to do with them: he can either use them to raise his own income and standard of living, or keep them in the firm in order to expand. On this decision will rest the whole future of the business.

It is not easy for the small firm to find long-term capital outside the business, and it is a hard but inescapable fact of life that for most small businesses growth is only possible if it can be financed largely from earnings retained in the business.

It is sometimes argued that this is no severe handicap. The argument runs: most small firms are highly self-financed, therefore they do not need to go outside the firm for funds. This merely confuses the issue, however: the truth is that most small firms are self-financed because they have to be, and firms have to wait for their savings to accumulate before they can grow. There is an alternative which is adopted by some growing firms, which is to finance growth partly by short- and medium-term credit; but this has its risks if not backed by internal finance, and in the last analysis it is not a substitute for savings.

How much to save and what proportion of earnings to put by depends on the circumstances of the firm; the strength of the desire to grow, the speed at which to grow, the sort of reserves, the excellence or otherwise of market possibilities and a host of other factors will affect the decision.

Small businesses have the handicap that they are frequently less profitable than large ones; it must be remembered, however, that part of this apparent lower profitability is due to the tendency for working proprietors to take out part of their share of profits as salaries or directors' fees, thus reducing the apparent size of profits.

Many small businesses could go a long way towards solving their financial problems by retaining more of their profits than they do. But motivation is important: many proprietors are content with what they take home at present, and are not anxious to take on the additional cares and responsibilities of growth; they might well ask why they should save more. It is inconsistent to hold this view and at the same time to suggest that it should be easier to get outside money, but it is a legitimate point of view for the individual, even if it does mean that it shows preference for a static company as against growth (and unfortunately, since things do not stand still, static usually means declining).

One way in which many small business could go some of the way to solving their financial problems is by becoming more profitable, thus generating more earnings for retention, and actually retaining the money when earned.

Responsible lending institutions tend to base their policy on the principle that the sound growth of a firm should be based largely on the adequate participation of its owners. And in the long run this participation can only come from savings, without which it is usually difficult to raise funds from outside sources.

CHAPTER 6

LONG-TERM CAPITAL*

SMALLER businesses have particular difficulties in the field of long-term capital; many of the problems are due simply to the scale of operation and financial requirements, but many others are due to the difficulties experienced by the smaller businesses in persuading potential lenders to put up money.

Capital issues are not a major source of funds for small private companies, and frequently the only significant issue of shares by a private company is that made when the company is first formed.

Private companies

The transformation from unincorporated business to private company status is one of the more important stages in the growth of a business; at a later stage "going public" may be even more important.

A private company may be formed for a variety of reasons, of which perhaps the most common is the need for capital for growth. But the move may be a mere change of legal form, the objective of which is to limit liabilities and risks; in this case the existing proprietors simply take their existing shares in the business as ordinary shares and become directors instead of partners or proprietors. The actual or imminent death of a partner may create difficulties: his heirs may either want to take their share in cash or as a major or controlling share in the business, neither of which may be acceptable to other owners. Similarly the incidence of death duty may leave existing partnerships in difficult circumstances which can only be overcome by the formation of a company (although even this may not completely overcome the difficulties); Estate Duties Investment Trust Ltd. (Edith) had its *raison d'être* in this problem.

Before the 1967 Companies Act "exempt" private company status had several appeals for the family concern, not least of which was the cherished privilege of not having to disclose its financial affairs (a privilege which is much less important than many proprietors

---

* References to the Bibliography are indicated, *e.g.* see *Bib.* 25; the Bibliography is to be found on pages 177–181.

imagine); under the 1967 Act private companies are no longer exempt from the requirement to file balance sheets, profit and loss accounts and other financial information with the Registrar of Companies. In Britain part of the price of limited liability is now the publication of some information about the business. The 1965 Finance Act also had an effect; it introduced corporation tax and Schedule F income tax payable at standard rate of income tax but with some discrimination between distributed and undistributed profits. These two changes in legislation have meant that private limited company status has fewer advantages than it had formerly, and businesses are less likely to adopt it for its own sake.

The formation of a private company is not particularly expensive and the legal procedure is relatively simple (but not a do-it-yourself job); a proportionate tax is paid on authorised capital and there are registration and stamp fees, but these do not amount to a large sum. The raising of further capital is facilitated—at the cost of the additional tax—if the company fixes authorised capital at a higher sum than it proposes to obtain at the time, since further share issues do not then require the formal consent of shareholders.

One of the more important reasons for the adoption of company status is the need for capital for growth. Potential lenders are commonly reluctant to put money into a partnership, whereas they may be willing either to take a share of the equity in, or to make a secured loan to, a company. There is a stage in the growth of most businesses when the change to company status becomes inevitable, and since the majority of owners of smaller businesses either do not want or cannot really afford to become public companies, private company status is the sensible thing to choose.

Going public

When larger sums of money are required, however, and when a satisfactory rate of growth is struck, public company status may well be considered. This is rarely worth while if less than half a million pounds is required, but there are exceptions to this rather crude generalisation. One of the main advantages of going public is that it enables the company to attract equity capital from a wide range of investors; this has the dual effect of widening the field from which the company can draw money and reducing its reliance on one or two large holders who may exercise a degree of control which the owners do not want. There is another advantage, that going public in effect advertises the business and may create a favourable image among customers, suppliers and potential lenders. One of the main considerations which stops many private companies from going public is the fear of loss of control; this danger can be reduced if existing owners are prepared to take up a substantial share of the new capital.

Of 570,000 companies having a share capital in 1967, 553,000 were private companies, but the private companies only accounted for just over a third of total paid up capital (see *Bib.* 25). From the end of the Second World War up to 1967, when the new Companies Act was passed, there was an increasing frequency of private company registrations. Since the disappearance of the exempt private company, there is a very slight tendency for the number of unlimited company registrations to increase (even so there were only 180 new registrations of unlimited companies in 1968 compared with 60 in the year before the 1967 Act came into force); in addition 2,640 companies re-registered as unlimited between the coming into force of the 1967 Act and the end of 1969 (*i.e.* less than one per cent. of the exempt companies in existence at the end of 1967). It is early yet to discern a trend but there are few signs so far of the disappearance of the private company.

The New Issue Market

The New Issue Market in Great Britain consists of a small group of issuing houses and merchant banks which specialise in the issue of new share capital; its prime function is to act as an intermediary between those who wish to invest in share capital and those who wish to raise it. The typical small business cannot use its facilities, but it can be very important to the business which wishes to adopt public company status. Some issuing houses are prepared occasionally to introduce private companies with good records and prospects to private individuals who are prepared to provide capital; as a rule this would be undertaken with a view to eventual flotation as a company, but there are occasions when this is not necessarily so. For the medium-sized growing company contact with an issuing house is frequently worth while even if no new issues are immediately contemplated; the houses also provide other services and advice on various financial matters such as capitalisation of reserves, amalgamation, dividend policy and so on, as well as nursing businesses along towards company status.

There are five main methods of share issue:

(1) the offer for sale;
(2) the issue by prospectus;
(3) the placing;
(4) the Stock Exchange introduction;
(5) the issue to shareholders.

In the case of an offer for sale an issuing houses buys the shares and offers them to the public. With an issue by prospectus the issuing house undertakes to find subscriptions for the issue. Neither of these methods is open to the private company, which is not permitted to invite public subscriptions. The private placing, which may be obtained either with or without a Stock Exchange quotation, is a method whereby the issuing house sells shares to brokers or jobbers and thence to private investors. The Stock Exchange introduction is effectively an application by the issuing house on behalf of the share-holders for shares to be quoted on a Stock Exchange. The issue to shareholders (sometimes called a rights issue if the company is public, since the existing shareholders receive preferential treatment) may be undertaken either within existing authorised capital limits or, if these are too restrictive, from an increase in authorised capital (which requires permission).

Forms of capital

Both loan and share capital involve the sale of some security by the business: share capital carries with it a share in the ownership or a prior right to a share of the profits; a loan carries a prior right to interest and normally over the assets as well. Share capital is never repayable, save by permission of the High Court; loan capital is repayable, but lenders cannot demand repayment before the term of the loan, although they may of course sell their holding.

Share capital may be of two main kinds: ordinary share capital normally carries a vote proportionate to the number of shares and receives its reward in the form of a dividend paid out of the income of the business after prior charges; preference shares do not usually carry a vote, but in compensation they have a prior right to dividend at a fixed rate. There are many variants of both types of share capital.

Non-cash issues of shares do not result in any new funds. A bonus issue is a free additional issue of shares to existing shareholders in proportion to their shareholding. It may be either a capitalisation of reserves or, less frequently, a capitalisation of current earnings; in either case it is a book-keeping transaction designed to make the liabilities side of the balance sheet correspond fairly closely to reality. Although both reserves and share capital are part of the net worth of a business (and therefore a liability to the shareholders) reserves may be distributed whereas share capital may not; if, by means of a bonus issue a transfer is made from reserves to share capital, this constitutes recognition that this capital is an essential part of the business and tied up in it. Non-cash issues may also be made in order to acquire other assets, such as trade investments, or for the purchase in whole or in part of another business. In general, however, non-cash issues are rare in smaller companies; indeed, they rarely make bonus issues quickly enough to increase their issued capital at the same rate as their net assets, and the rate of issued capital to reserves in many older small companies is frequently too low.

Long-term liabilities are of two main types: mortgage debentures and floating-charge debentures. With the first type the security offered is usually in the form of the buildings of the company; with the second type no particular or specified assets form the security but the debenture holders have a prior claim on all of the company's assets in the event of liquidation. Occasionally an unsecured loan may be obtained, but this is uncommon.

Mortgages are usually provided either by insurance companies or investment companies, and are usually repayable over a specified period by direct payments or insurance. Insurance companies usually prefer loans of over £20,000 and of up to 70 per cent. of the value of the property; endowment policies may also be involved, and there may also be a requirement that all general insurance business is done with the company. Naturally enough insurance companies require good security, and the property itself may not be sufficient; they frequently require, for example, some evidence that the earning capacity of the business will justify the loan and be adequate to service it. The mortgage raised on business property is similar to the mortgage on the house of the private individual; the main difference is that the building society (as distinct from the insurance company) is not usually prepared to lend on business premises and is rarely interested in large loans.

Generally speaking, in order to obtain a long-term loan a company must offer the lender a reasonable prospect of good and stable earnings in the future, and its assets must be realisable if the enterprise should fail. From the point of view of the ordinary shareholders there are two contingent risks in debentures: first is that they commit the assets of the business and may leave little over for the shareholders; second is that they add to fixed interest charges.

Renting

It is possible to obtain substantial economies of capital by renting or leasing buildings, and if premises represent a large proportion of the capital needs of a business, this possibility becomes increasingly attractive. It is not always easy to obtain suitable rented property, but for the newer business it is frequently worth while to look around, particularly in areas, such as development areas, where special provision is made for renting of factory buildings as part of packages for the inducement of industry. In the early stages of the life of a business it is more likely than not that renting of buildings will be the best way of acquiring them; later on it may be worth while buying them. The established business may also be in a position to move to rented property, but this is a major decision not to be taken too lightly; alternatively, it may sell its buildings to an institution such as an insurance company and lease them back, and where such arrangements are possible (and they rarely are for very small or specific buildings) it may well be preferable to the alternative of trying to arrange a mortgage on the property. Putting the renting proposition in its simplest terms, there are profitable opportunities if the business can obtain a greater return from its capital by putting it to other uses, provided that the expected returns from these other uses are greater than the costs of renting the buildings (after making due allowance for improvements in site values, etc.); it is merely one more lease-or-buy decision.

Some specific problems

The majority of small businesses only require relatively small sums for expansion, and it may be too expensive to raise these through the traditional sources of long-term external funds. For example, the costs of small issues of capital are high: they contain a large overhead element in advertising, printing of a prospectus and so on, and if a quotation is required this too can be expensive. Henderson (see *Bib.* 46) showed, for example, that the cost of small private placings was in the order of 24 per cent., for small offers and public issues the cost was 11·5 per cent., larger placings cost 9 per cent. and larger issues cost 7·6 per cent.

The costs are higher for the company which comes to the market for the first time, and costs of issues by established quoted companies tend to be lower both in relative and absolute terms. The private placing and the issue to shareholders are really the only source of new share capital for the private company unless it is prepared to become a public company; even the private placing is difficult because few investors are keen on buying securities which are not readily marketable, unless the profit prospects are remarkably good or there is some additional incentive such as a share in the control of the business.

Shares in private companies are neither marketable nor easily transferable, and this reduces their attractiveness to investors. In-stitutional investors are rarely keen to buy shares which cannot readily be sold, and many private investors also like to feel that they can opt out when they wish; institutional investors such as unit trusts, pension funds, insurance companies and so on are becoming increasingly important buyers and sellers on stock markets, and growing dependence on them makes things more difficult for the smaller company. The difficulty is increased by the dislike of such investors for small holdings (under £10,000); this dislike is largely due to the cost and difficulties of administration of small holdings.

Things are not made any easier by the fact that shares in private companies may only be transferred at the discretion of the directors.

Many of the difficulties of the smaller business are due to owner-ship problems: many forms of long-term finance carry with them a share in the ownership of the business. Many owners of small busi-nesses are reluctant to part with any share of the ownership at all, and even those whose pride of ownership or possession is weaker are not keen to see sufficient of the equity owned by outsiders to offer any threat to their own control. But if they are not to be offered any say in running the business, many outside investors not unnaturally are not interested in putting money into it (this reluctance is strengthened by the fact that they cannot get rid of their shares easily if they want to get out). Thus the owners of many small businesses simply have to face up to the fact that they have a choice: if they want extra long-term capital they may have to give up a bit of the owner-ship of the company or be prepared to match new funds with money of their own; if they are not prepared to do so they cannot want the funds so very badly. The problem need not arise in so stark a form: some of the newer institutions are not particularly keen on acquiring a very large stake in the businesses in which they invest, and do indeed argue that it is not their business to go into the management of small concerns.

If ownership were all that mattered the majority of companies would seek to meet their long-term financial needs through forms which did not raise ownership problems, and would probably opt for preference shares or debentures since neither of these impairs or endangers the existing controlling interest. But preference shares are not particularly attractive to potential investors in a small business, and too heavy a reliance on debentures may not look so good on the balance sheet when further funds are needed. In practice many other considerations are important.

The first of these is gearing (or leverage as it is known in the United States). Strictly the gearing of a company is represented by the ratio of the annual amount payable on prior charges and fixed interest (*i.e.* preference and debenture interest) to annual income for disposal. Thus, if annual fixed interest payments are £25,000, and disposable income is £50,000, such a gearing ratio would be 50 per cent.; if disposable income was £250,000 in the same company in another year, the ratio would only be 10 per cent. In good times, when profits are high, therefore, the gearing problem is less serious than in bad times when profits are low, because in the former case the fixed interest commitments are less of a burden on the earned income of the business. It is of course extremely difficult to predict profitability, and a perfectly adequate guide to gearing may be obtained from the ratio of fixed interest capital to ordinary capital, taking the nominal value of the respective shares and stocks; another commonly calculated capitalisation ratio expresses fixed interest capital as a percentage of equity shareholders' interest in the concern (ordinary share capital plus reserves).

High gearing is not only a burden on the firm itself. It may also deter outside investors, who would be reluctant to invest in a business which had heavy fixed interest commitments; as potential ordinary shareholders they would fear that insufficient would be left for them, whilst as potential preference shareholders they might fear that dividends were inadequately covered. Generally speaking, small companies in the United Kingdom are not highly geared; Boswell (see

Bib. 21) did note that businesses assisted by ICFC were more highly geared than quoted public companies, but his gearing calculations included bank overdrafts as part of long-term capital. His argument is interesting: he treats bank borrowing as part of capital employed and not as a current liability, on the grounds that ICFC customers tend to have tapped bank credit to the full and it is therefore realistic to treat bank borrowing as stable and continuing. "For this reason ICFC strongly adheres to the view that on balance it is wiser, and a better test for management, to include bank borrowing in the 'capital employed' or overall financial resources used by a firm." It is an interesting idea, and the owners of many small businesses might sensibly think of overdraft interest as a continuing commitment, and take it into account in their gearing calculations.

The outside investor might also express interest in another capital-isation ratio: that of total current and long-term liabilities to tangible net worth, which shows the relationship between the owners' stake and the investment of outsiders. If this ratio is more than one, it means that outsiders may have too big a stake in the business, and lenders could well be concerned about the relatively low security afforded by the owners.

Few outside investors are prepared to put their money into a business unless there is adequate equity participation by existing owners; the reason for this is quite simply that they like to be assured that the owners have some stake and interest in the efficient running and success of the business. The owners who have backed themselves with their own money, either from the beginning or through the retention of profits, are likely to be looked on much more favourably than those who keep their stake to a minimum from the start and fail to plough back money into the business; this is particularly true in the case of the smaller business with no long record of profitability. Added to which, of course, the ordinary shareholders are legally liable for the debts of the company only up to the limit of their shareholding.

In general, reluctance to surrender equity or a share of it is a serious limitation on the smaller business, and the expansion of many concerns is held back by the inability of its owners to take a sufficient share in the growth. The raising of both long- and short-term funds is made more difficult.

In addition, the past success and future prospects of many small companies depends on one or two personalities in the business: they may have difficulty in demonstrating their own potential; they may also find it difficult to persuade a lender that the business could carry on in the event of their death (*i.e.* management succession may be inadequately provided for).

Even the new issue to shareholders is of little help in many companies. It is a cheap method, since it may be brought to the notice of shareholders by means of a circular, and it requires neither advertising nor prospectus. Shareholders are normally invited to subscribe in proportion to their present shareholdings, but in the private company which is limited to fifty shareholders it is always likely that many shareholders would not be able to accept the invitation. Since the field of influence of the private company in this sense is small, there is a severe limit to the amount of money which this sort of issue is likely to yield.

The field of influence of the small private company is also likely to be restricted to the locality within which it works and the trade within which it operates, and it is not easy to get beyond this fairly narrow circle to raise money.

But even when it is possible to go beyond this immediate field the family company and the director-controlled company in particular have further problems: they may themselves be unable to put up enough money to take an adequate share of the new issue, with the consequences of potential loss of control or failure to interest outside lenders because of inadequate participation.

Preference shares are not very attractive to smaller businesses; although they do not involve dangers of loss of control, it is never easy to find buyers for them and in any case, as against debentures they are less attractive from the tax point of view, since interest on debentures is allowable as a cost against tax whereas dividends on preference shares are not. The great disadvantage of debentures on the other hand is that they represent a charge on the company's assets and may adversely affect borrowing on short term from banks and others; but a great deal depends on who holds the debentures and on what proportion they are of total long-term capital.

The Radcliffe Committee (see *Bib.* 72; p. 80 of Report) summed up another limitation of the smaller business:

"It is implicit in the situation of a rapidly growing small firm that it cannot offer altogether adequate security for the loan capital that it wants and cannot afford to borrow without some assurance that it will not be asked to make early repayment."

It may be argued that a private company can overcome many of these difficulties by becoming a public company, but such a step may be too all-embracing and expensive for the small growth contemplated by many businesses.

Businesses in the Oxford Survey rarely made new issues of long-term capital, and when they did they tended to be small and were mainly made to shareholders. There is no evidence to suggest that anything different has been happening in more recent years, and effectively new share issues are still a relatively unimportant source of funds for the established private companies.

Alternative sources and institutions

The difficulty of the private company in its search for long-term capital funds, and the rarity of capital issues was recognised by the Macmillan Committee (see *Bib*. 58) and stressed again by the Radcliffe Committee (see *Bib*. 72).

The Macmillan Report recommended the setting up of a company to devote itself to the smaller industrial and commercial issues, but it was several years before any positive action was taken. Despite many efforts to fill this gap, the Radcliffe Committee still had to report in 1959:

"There is . . . no recognised and readily accessible channel corresponding to the new issue market for large firms, through which the small industrialist can raise long-term funds. There is only a list of institutions, of which he and his advisers may or may not know or get to hear, and who may or may not be willing to lend when approached. There is no escape from this problem, which is inherent in the smallness or the nature of the borrowing concern. . . ."

There have been improvements in recent years in the facilities available for the provision of long-term funds for both large and small concerns. The new issue market, for example, has devoted more attention to home issues, in contrast to the earlier situation in which issuing houses were largely concerned with issues on behalf of overseas borrowers. Although the Issuing Houses Association said in their memorandum of evidence to the Radcliffe Committee (see *Bib*. 72; p. 80 of Report) that the amount of new money raised through the market was marginal in relation to the total flow of capital investment in the private sector of the economy, the Committee disagreed and said:

". . . the new issue market has been a far from marginal source of capital in the calculation of most of the larger firms."

In the absence of facilities for raising long-term capital private companies have come to depend for their funds on internal sources and short- and medium-term sources of funds, and it is often argued that this has been a brake on the expansion of small concerns. One consequence of the attention given to the need for some alternative sources analogous to the new issue market has been the growth in recent years of a number of specialist institutions whose aim has been to provide capital for the financing of small business.

The first to be set up was the Charterhouse organisation, which was originally conceived as a nursery for private companies, the aim being to provide promising firms with finance until the time comes for a public issue; over the years the aim has changed rather and the Charterhouse group has become more of an institutional investor with many minority shareholdings in private companies. The difficulties of this position—the most notable of which is the dilemma between the owners' desire to avoid 51 per cent. of equity participation by an outside institution and the institution's reluctance to place itself in the position of a minority shareholder with no say— seem to have been overcome fairly successfully by the Charterhouse group.

The next large organisation to be set up was the Industrial and Commercial Finance Corporation (ICFC), which came into existence in 1945 with a nominal capital of £15 million, subscribed by the Bank of England and the clearing banks. Powers to borrow a further £30 million from the shareholding banks were granted, and in 1959 the Corporation was granted permission to make debenture issues in the market. At March 31, 1969, ICFC had a share capital of £40 million, and debenture stocks of £70 million.

ICFC is prepared to find finance in the form of secured or unsecured loans, debentures or share capital. Loans are normally repaid over ten to twenty years, the instalments being arranged to suit the particular case; rates of interest are in line with current commercial rates, although a fixed rate is usually quoted for the entire period of the loan. Propositions are usually investigated in some detail, and ICFC has a staff of specialist engineers, accountants and economists.

After the initial inquiry the Corporation requires more detailed information from the client. This will include: an estimate of total finance required; the way in which the finance will be used, and specific amounts required for such items as buildings, plant, working capital, etc.; the proportion of new finance which will be provided by existing shareholders; a history of the business; a copy of accounts for several years back showing turnover and profits; and a description of the nature of the business, its products, customers, sales, prospects, etc.

In an *Announcement to the Public* at the time of its formation in 1945, it was stated that the Corporation would "... supplement, but not supersede, the activities of other lenders as financial institutions." Of £125 million outstanding at March 31, 1969, 56·4 per cent. was in the form of loans, 13·2 per cent. in preference or preferred ordinary shares, 15·7 per cent. in ordinary shares, 3·3 per cent. in leased property and equipment, and 11·4 per cent. in a highly specialised activity, ships under charter.

ICFC has made a valuable contribution to the problem of providing long-term funds for small business. In the first twenty years of its life, ICFC provided finance for some 2,000 smaller companies, most of them owner-managed.

A major limitation in its early days was the size of transaction in which ICFC might engage: it was considered at the time of the Corporation's inception that small sums (under £5,000) could be provided by the banks, and sums over £200,000 could be provided by the new issue market; the evidence of Lord Piercy, the Chairman of ICFC, to the Radcliffe Committee (see *Bib.* 72; p. 327 of Report) implied that but for this limitation ICFC would on occasion take part in issues of £300,000 to £400,000. This particular limitation may not be quite so restrictive now. Of £125 million outstanding at March 31, 1969, 17·9 per cent. was in respect of amounts less than £50,000, and 19·3 per cent. was for amounts greater than £300,000 (of which there were forty-seven instances).

For several years the resources of ICFC were probably too small but in recent years there has been a rearrangement of its finances, the import of which has been that nowadays ICFC draws its additional resources from the capital market in the form of debentures instead of relying, as hitherto, on the commercial banks. This means that the Corporation's borrowing is now more expensive, and has a larger long-term fixed interest element; on the other hand, the Corporation's borrowing is now on a longer-term basis, and ICFC is more free than it was of the possibility of control by the banks.

Boswell (see *Bib.* 21) showed that the majority of companies assisted by ICFC started with net assets of less than £250,000 and most of them had fewer than 500 employees; the majority were in manufacturing, with an emphasis on engineering. In terms of financial characteristics, the 300 businesses surveyed by Boswell had, by comparison with quoted public companies, higher stocks and work in progress, heavier reliance on trade and bank credit, and a greater proportion of post-tax profits retained in the business; they were also less liquid and had less quickly realisable current assets. They came

TABLE 22

ICFC FINANCIAL FACILITIES OUTSTANDING, MARCH 31, 1969

Amount	Customers		Aggregate Amount	
	No.	%	£'000	%
Up to £10,000	425	22·7	2,223	1·8
£10,001–£20,000	326	17·4	4,461	3·6
£20,001–£50,000	490	26·2	15,669	12·5
£50,001–£100,000	306	16·4	21,446	17·2
£100,001–£200,000	198	10·6	27,310	21·8
£200,001–£300,000	68	3·6	15,548	12·4
£300,001 and over	47	2·5	24,194	19·3
	1,860	99·4	110,851	88·6
Ships under charter	12	0·6	14,239	11·4
	1,872	100·0	125,090	100·0

Source: ICFC, *Twenty-Fourth Annual Report* 1968–69, Table 5.

to ICFC because they had got beyond the point where they could finance their development from existing sources but had not got anywhere near the stage of access to the new issue market; they were anxious not to lose control. ICFC assistance was mainly directed to capital expenditure (60–65 per cent.), with a smaller proportion going to the financing of working capital, and an even smaller proportion going to such miscellaneous purposes as the funding of "hard-core" overdrafts, helping shareholders to retain control, death duties and financial reorganisation. Typically, ICFC finance accounted for 12–15 per cent. of capital employed in the companies. The companies assisted by ICFC tended to grow rather more rapidly than quoted companies, and tended to be more profitable; this goes to show that ICFC knows how to pick a winner, and when it does help, its assistance is invaluable. Whether it fills the Macmillan Gap is another matter; there are thousands of other businesses, many of which are likely to be of similar potential and it is doubtful whether ICFC or any other organisation could meet the needs of them all.

It is frequently said in criticism that ICFC is not sufficiently adventurous; but in a sense this misunderstands the function of ICFC, which is to seek out credit-worthy concerns and not to be an adventurer. ICFC may not have gone far enough in its search for credit-worthy firms, and may possibly insist too much on ordinary standards of credit-worthiness, but it is in business to make a profit, and it does use up-to-date techniques of planning and financial evaluation. It is reasonable to enforce normal standards, and most lending institutions have to take a prudent if far-sighted view, but one of the problems of small firms is that they frequently cannot fulfil normal standards: they may not have a good profit record, they may appear risky, their plans take a long time to mature. They may not appeal to the traditional lenders, and may not be able to offer the security normally required, or to demonstrate their long-term prospects, however good they may be. Without offering indiscriminate charity, such firms may well benefit from more generous lending policies; whether ICFC should do the job, or indeed whether the community can afford to devote its resources to such uses, is of course a different matter.

A factor inhibiting the scope of operations of ICFC in early years was the unwillingness of borrowers to approach the Corporation. The owners of many small firms fear loss of independence if they accept help from ICFC: these fears are unrealistic, and ICFC never tries to obtain voting control of companies in which it takes an interest, though it may well appoint a director to the board, and gives advice on technical and financial matters. This means that ICFC has little legal protection against incompetence or sharp practice, and its success depends on careful choice of companies (another factor which probably restricts its lending).

Furthermore, many small firms simply do not know of the existence of ICFC, or confuse it with other organisations (the initials are similar to those of at least two private organisations which have vastly different aims and policies); and this ignorance persists despite wide advertising and other efforts to make the Corporation known. And unfortunately, ICFC probably gets at least as many bad potential clients among businessmen as it gets good ones: satisfied clients may well not say much, but rejected applicants (and 80 per cent. of applications are turned down) tend to be very vocal and bitter about their rejection.

In short, ICFC is a highly successful and widely admired financial institution which provides invaluable help to a number of companies; it specialises in helping small companies, and has an enviable record for picking the good ones. In twenty-five years it has become an integral part of the British financial system.

In 1952 another industrial investor specialising in private company finance entered the field. This was the Estate Duties Investment Trust Ltd. (EDITH), which specialises in investments in private companies whose market for securities is restricted and where there is a difficulty in disposing of shares. Capital for EDITH was subscribed by institutional investors, including ICFC, by insurance companies and investment trusts. Finance is not usually supplied direct, but the investment is most frequently undertaken by the acquisition of a capital issue from existing shareholders; ordinary or preference shares may be acquired. The aim is usually to provide money for the present or expected payment of estate duties, and to preserve for the company the protection of limited liability and restricted transferability of shares, but EDITH does not restrict its activities to such cases; financial assistance has been mainly to medium-sized rather than small businesses.

Other institutional investors do this sort of business. Some investment trust companies will invest in unquoted securities, but only under conditions which will make the investment attractive. Amounts of less than £20,000 are rarely invested in this way, although initially the sum may be smaller and businesses chosen are usually those which may be expected to become viable in a relatively short period (up to five years): businesses of a technical nature are sometimes preferred. If an investment trust does put money into a small firm it may well be prepared to sacrifice income in early years in exchange for capital appreciation of ordinary shares: this has the advantage that capital does not have to be serviced in early years. But investment trusts may well ask for some share of control, and in any case are rarely interested in the very small firm.

Several other institutions have turned their attention to the problem of financing small firms in the thirty years or so since the Macmillan Report; some investment companies, merchant banks and combinations of institutional investors form "industrial holdings," which provide long-term capital to firms in which they hold majority or substantial equity interests, but it is not usual to find that such investors are interested in more than a limited number of small firms.

The facilities available were described in evidence before the Radcliffe Committee (see *Bib.* 72; p. 324 of Report) by Lord Piercy:

"They are not non-existent, but they are miscellaneous, dispersed and not very obvious to the industrialist, or his advisers. Mere bald enumeration does less than justice to their variety, nor can an enumeration be exhaustive; but they include:

"1. Insurance companies for mortgages on industrial property and certain other types of capital loans and for purchase and lease-back facilities, often associated with the placing of the borrower's insurance business with the lending company; this source must be rated in the aggregate as important.

"2. A few investment trusts for an occasional investment in an unquoted security. Though there is one group of investment trusts which, as a policy, has invested substantially in unquoted securities this source cannot be rated as significant.

"3. Some merchant bankers, finance houses and stockbrokers, for an occasional investment—typically for developing a new idea or a novel venture. Not much weight of money from these quarters.

"4. One or two issuing houses for loans to unquoted companies by way of 'nursing' them for a comparatively near issue. Not very important and prima facie very selective.

"5. Sundry suppliers or customers in industry for occasional loans made with the object of tying a connection."

The last-named is the remaining source of long-term funds for consideration. It is sometimes possible to obtain finance for buying or extending a business from a manufacturer or a supplier. Some brewery companies, foodstuff manufacturers and the major oil companies will make loans for public-houses, shops and garages; and in the opposite situation some large retail organisations will provide finance for manufacturers supplying them with goods. The major danger associated with this form of finance is that of domination by the supplier of credit: sometimes restrictive terms are included in the agreement and the borrower may be denied discounts and access to other suppliers; and it is by no means uncommon for such loans to lead eventually to absorption by the lender.

The experience of the Oxford Survey suggests that few small businesses really make much of an effort to get properly based long-term funds; over 90 per cent. of respondents in that survey had not tried to get finance from specialised institutions. About half of them had never even heard of any such institutions; those who had heard of them did not want anything to do with such institutions, usually because they did not want any outside interference with their business. Those who said this were no doubt misinformed and misunderstood the purpose of the institutions, but this was their feeling, and this feeling is very important in that it does affect the availability of finance to the small firms. If these institutions are to be criticised it is because they have not succeeded in dispelling notions about their aims and policies. Many of the businesses which had sought such funds had done so because they were in difficulties from which they needed extracting in order to avoid collapse (difficulties probably caused by inefficiency in many cases), whereas the aim of such institutions is the more positive one of helping expansion.

For reasons why companies do not seek outside funds, the replies given in the Oxford Survey (Table 23) are as valid now as they were then.

TABLE 23

REASONS FOR NOT TRYING OUTSIDE SOURCES
OF FUNDS [1]

	Number of Firms
No need to, satisfied with present situation	512
Use own profits, or directors provide funds	98
Want to keep business from outside interference	66
Don't like loans, wish to avoid debt	38
Interest too high	7
Prefer overdraft (cheaper; bank always helps)	47
Difficulty or cost of issuing shares	1
Have other sources (*e.g.* parent company or associated companies)	24
Waste of time trying because we would not get it	16
Other reasons (*e.g.* labour shortage, no wish to grow, prefers to approach commercial sources)	22
Don't know	133
Did consider and did try	125
	1,089

[1] These reasons are not mutually exclusive.

Summing up

Small businesses rarely raise any long-term capital after their initial establishment; this is largely due to what Lord Piercy called the "bar of size" in the new issue market (see *Bib.* 72; p. 81 of Report). Perhaps the growing importance of institutional investors in the

market has made things more difficult, since in a general way they do
not like small holdings because of the difficulty of administration and
do not like unquoted securities because of their lack of marketability.
Apart from this, when rising prices are discounted, it is doubtful
whether the market has become more difficult in recent years, but the
new issue market itself has certainly not improved from the point of
view of the small business.

The Radcliffe Committee (see *Bib.* 72; p. 82 of Report) commented:

"It is possible that most of the smaller issues are made by companies with
assets well in excess of £250,000; but we are inclined to think that, if the
facilities of the new issue market now seem less adequate to the needs of the
smaller firms, the explanation lies in the fact that more people are trying to
borrow rather than in any greater difficulty in floating small issues."

What is perhaps more surprising is that very little use is made by
small firms of the other and newer institutional sources of funds. It is
very likely that this is due in large measure to the ignorance on the
part of the businessmen of the existence of such sources, and that in
any case many of the smaller firms are not sufficiently credit-worthy
to be good candidates for funds: ideally, however, one would like to
feel that these institutions were genuinely filling a gap and that more
use was being made of them.

The Radcliffe Committee (see *Bib.* 72; p. 325 of Report) said:

"We do not propose that there should be a proliferation of institutions,
whether financed by public or private money, to provide finance for small
businesses. On the contrary we believe that, with certain modifications . . .
the existing institutions can look after the ordinary requirements of small
businesses for capital. But it is important that bank managers, solicitors, and
accountants who are the professional advisers of small businesses should be
well informed about the existing institutions and what they have to offer."

Perhaps the institutions themselves could help by making themselves better known, and by making an attempt to clear up miscon-
ceptions on the part of businessmen, and they could probably do
more if they had bigger resources.

For the company which can offer sound prospects, however, there
are sources of long-term capital available and things are a great deal
better now than they were in the 1930s and early post-war period
when the Macmillan gap was wider than it is now. In addition to the
newer institutions, the insurance companies, the merchant banks and

other organisations will all provide long-term finance in one form or another for certain purposes. Some provide funds for the exploitation of innovations and for technologically based developments; they are special cases which are considered later (Chap. 9). But they do not all provide the same services and to some extent it is up to the borrower to decide which of them will provide the best solution to his problems; they are not, however, last resorts after the businessman has exhausted all other possibilities.

There are few reliable guidelines to the smaller business which seeks to raise long-term external finance. The financial adviser to such a company might, however, make suggestions along the following lines:

(a) Sound long-term financial planning is essential; a potential lender will want to know what the money is needed for (capital equipment, working capital, funding of bank loans, etc.); he will also expect to see reasonable cash-flow forecasts, market assessments (including possibly breakdowns of sales and profits by products, lists of important customers, etc.) and audited statements for recent years.

(b) Long-term needs should be financed from long-term capital and not from short-term sources.

(c) It is essential to know *how much* money is wanted.

(d) Outside lenders will rarely put money into a business in which the owners' present and projected future equity participation is considered inadequate.

(e) A good profit record is a good recommendation.

(f) Help is unlikely to be provided for a sinking ship, or when things have been left too late.

(g) Leases, much bank borrowing and loans from individuals may be treated by the lender as part of the long-term debt structure of the business.

(h) Special cases, such as technological innovations or developments, exports, or something which would go well in a development area, may be better financed from specialised sources.

(i) Good management is the main thing that long-term lenders will back.

CHAPTER 7

BANK CREDIT*

BANK loans are the traditional source of short-term funds for business, and they provide a large share of the financing of both large and small businesses. Bankers are usually not quite so hard on their smaller customers as they are frequently held up to be, and indeed many a small business owes its life to bank support at crucial times. But bank overdrafts, which account for the major part of bank lending, are short-term and, even if it were possible, it would be unwise to try to finance longer-term needs from this source.

British banks traditionally do not consider the provision of long-term funds for industry to be part of their business, but concentrate in the main on the financing of short-term needs. This is in direct contrast with German banks, which do take part in long-term lending and have a large stake in the finance and indeed in the running of German industry. Occasionally, however, within limits, they are prepared to offer some long-term funds; there are signs that in recent years, when not held back by Government credit policy, they have been lending an increasing amount on rather longer term than has hitherto been considered normal. But in general this sort of business is exceptional for the banks, who prefer to finance increases in working capital, the need for which arises with the increasing need for, stocks, debtors' accounts, etc., associated with a growing concern.

The Radcliffe Report (see *Bib.* 72) said:

"The joint stock banks are very important in the finance of small businesses, not only as a major source of capital but because the ordinary business of banking establishes a close contact between businessmen and bank managers which puts the bank manager in a unique position to help and advise the businessman on his financial affairs. The evidence which we have heard from the representatives of the banks and from branch bank managers make it clear that banks recognise that small concerns stand in special need of their support and help them to the best of their ability. It is evident too, that though the bank advance is conventionally a short-term loan, the banks do in fact lend on a large scale to such customers to finance

---

* References to the Bibliography are indicated, *e.g.* see *Bib.* 25; the Bibliography is to be found on pages 177–181.

medium-term and long-term requirements. Indeed, at the time when the ICFC was set up, the banks publicly expressed their determination to help 'small traders', and said that in this connection they would 'have regard to economic justification rather than to the probable duration of an advance when considering applications for credit for small or moderate accounts.' Bank overdrafts are, however, legally repayable on demand and in practice subject to review annually: and it seems that some borrowers consider that, because they fear that the annual review may sometimes lead to a request for reduction of the overdraft, bank credit is too unreliable a form of credit for medium- or long-term purposes.

The stake of the joint stock banks in the financing of British industry may be judged from Table 24; £7,587 million were outstanding in 1969, of which about 40 per cent. was to manufacturing industry.

It is difficult to estimate how much of total bank lending goes to smaller businesses. R. F. Henderson (see *Bib.* 83) estimated that in 1949–1953 about 40 per cent. of total bank advances went to quoted public companies, the rest going mainly to other companies, private and professional people and the nationalised industries. An order-of-magnitude calculation suggests that bank advances to the non-quoted company sector of Britain are of the order of £1,500 million in 1970; it is impossible to say how much of this is to private companies, but perhaps in total somewhere between £700 million and £1,000 million is outstanding on loan to smaller businesses, including unincorporated businesses, in distribution, manufacturing and other production. But this is a hazardous figure.

Bank credit and the banker

The banker is in business as a commercial undertaking, using money deposited with him on short term and making profits from lending it. He will therefore require that any loan which he will make must fill three basic requirements: first is safety, which means that he requires security, but not necessarily physical security; second is liquidity, which means that he can recall if it is necessary, and he will only therefore lend it where he expects to be able to do this; third is profitability, which means that he will only lend if he expects that the borrower will be able to make profitable use of it and be able to pay the interest without difficulty.

A bank manager will therefore want to know about the history, structure of assets and liabilities, and profit record of a business

TABLE 24

ANALYSIS OF BANK ADVANCES TO UNITED KINGDOM RESIDENTS,
NOVEMBER 1969 [1]

Industry	Advances (£ million) [2]
Manufacturing	
Food, drink and tobacco	366·0
Chemicals and allied industries	236·6
Metal manufacture	169·9
Electrical engineering	390·3
Other engineering and metal goods	635·3
Shipbuilding	181·1
Vehicles	394·8
Textiles, leather and clothing	280·4
Other manufacturing	404·4
TOTAL MANUFACTURING	3,058·8
Other Production	
Agriculture, forestry and fishing	527·0
Mining and quarrying	95·4
Construction	371·5
TOTAL OTHER PRODUCTION	993·9
Financial	
Hire purchase finance companies	106·1
Property companies	322·8
U.K. banks	67·6
Other financial	439·5
TOTAL FINANCIAL	936·0
Services	
Transport and communication	225·4
Public utilities and national government	69·8
Local government services	66·0
Retail distribution	350·0
Other distribution	465·9
Professional, scientific and miscellaneous services	548·9
TOTAL SERVICES	1,726·0
Personal	
House purchase	378·7
Other personal	494·1
TOTAL PERSONAL	872·8
TOTAL TO U.K. RESIDENTS	7,587·5

[1] Source, *Bank of England Quarterly Bulletin*, Vol. 10, No. 1, March 1970, Table 11.
[2] Excluding figures for Northern Ireland banks (£145 million in total).

when assessing its eligibility for a loan. It is usual to ask for audited balance sheets and profit and loss accounts for several years past; nowadays the more progressive bank manager will also want some information on the expected cash flow of the business. From the balance sheet he will want to estimate the worth or earning capacity of the concern *after* current liabilities have been met, but he will rarely accept the balance-sheet valuations. Fictitious and intangible assets will be ignored, investments in subsidiaries treated with caution, tangible assets will be looked at from the point of view of what they would be worth if sold, stock valuations will be questioned, more information will be needed about debtors and creditors and the demands on the business, and so on. Other things looked for will be an adequate stake of the owners and a sensible ratio of current assets to liabilities. And, although the bank will not usually want any part of the running of the business, the customer has to be prepared to keep the bank fully informed of his financial position through annual and special periodic accounts.

Security for longer-term loans is usually required in the form of some of the company's assets, which may be those which are to be bought with the loans; the bank may also require a fixed charge or a mortgage on the assets. In the case of overdrafts less tangible security may be required and the bank manager will base his advance on his assessment of the credit-worthiness and profitability of the firm, although if these are in doubt he may still require a fixed or floating charge. Sometimes guarantees may be required from owners, directors or outside persons.

Businesses which have large quantities of stocks of raw materials may use a method known as *hypothecation of stocks*, whereby the bank will make an advance on the security of the stock held in bond (movements into and out of the bond being recorded and periodically notified to the bank).

The rate of interest charged is usually closely related to current Bank Rate, but varies according to the credit rating of the customer and the size of his account. Typically the terms are between $\frac{3}{4}$ and $1\frac{1}{2}$ per cent. above Bank Rate, with a minimum of $4\frac{1}{2}$–$5\frac{1}{2}$ per cent.

On the occasions when banks do lend money on a longer term they usually require some form of regular payment plan over the period; overdrafts are not usually subject to such repayment terms.

Once an overdraft is granted and the banker is satisfied that the business is a good customer, it is rarely withdrawn. Overdrafts are usually reviewed half yearly, but in practice it is not uncommon for them to run on for very long periods: if the business is maintaining or increasing its profitability the bank will usually be pleased to continue to lend, and at the same time will raise no objection to the business reinvesting its profits and acquiring new assets. In this sense the overdraft may facilitate if it does not actually finance the acquisition of assets which would normally require long-term capital; it should still not be treated as a source of long-term funds, however.

Bank credit provides a further illustration of the usefulness of sound planning and internal financial control. Borrowing from a bank is always easier if the businessman can indicate to the bank manager in advance that a loan will be needed: good budgets show this and also tell the bank manager that the firm is not trying to borrow merely because it is in difficulties but because of a conscious intention to grow and an awareness of what is involved.

It is sometimes said that banks will lend to anyone provided that they do not actually need the money. This is not entirely true, but it is true that a bank, by its very nature, has to lend most of its money to those who are in a strong financial position or who possess suitable security, or who can offer reasonable prospects of success and profitability.

An interesting development in the field of bank lending followed a recommendation of the Radcliffe Committee that, in view of the restrictive effect of the short-term nature of the ordinary bank loan, the banks might consider the practicability of introducing a scheme of "term loans," at a fixed rate of interest, and repayable, either over a period of time or at a given date in full. Such loans are common in the United States and Canada, but were virtually unknown in Britain until December 1959 when the Midland Bank (and the Clydesdale and North of Scotland Bank, its subsidiary) introduced such a scheme for loans of three to five years' duration. The other banks did not follow suit, and many bankers said there was no need for such a scheme since the ordinary overdraft schemes and personal loans were perfectly adequate, which misunderstands or misinterprets the points made by the Radcliffe Committee. The Midland Bank scheme was put into "temporary abeyance" during the Credit Squeeze of 1961 and has not formally been reinstated.

In recent years a number of the major American banks have been expanding their operations in the United Kingdom, and are offering competition to the British joint-stock banks. One form of competition is term-lending, to which American banks are accustomed and in which they are expert: one problem which might face British banks in this field is that term-lending is more specialised, and few branch managers would have the expertise; this might mean that such loans were best dealt with centrally, with a consequent loss of speed and personal contact. They are also more inclined to lend on prospects than on assets, or security, and are thus in direct contrast with much of traditional British banking; this is a fundamental difference in attitude, since the financing of prospects requires more dynamic criteria of credit-worthiness, and it is entirely good for British business.

Another related characteristic of the American banks is their insistence on cash-flow estimates wherever they are feasible; this too can produce nothing but good for the borrower, who is forced to plan and to recognise the implications of his plans.

The ideas of the banking profession on their role as business financiers have undergone vast changes in the last generation. Bankers will now consider propositions and advance funds on projects which were formerly thought to be completely outside the range of business of the joint stock bank. And they are far from indifferent to the problems of the small firms which still lie beyond their scope: witness their participation in the foundation of ICFC.

Bank borrowing and the individual firm

From the point of view of the firm the main disadvantage of the overdraft is its short duration, which makes it potentially unreliable and therefore unsuitable for longer-term finance.

But bank credit is a very convenient form of finance for the firm with a good standing at the bank. Since bank managers are extremely wary of the possibility of bad debts, however, many firms cannot avail themselves of overdrafts. Bank managers want to know a great deal about a firm; but in new firms which obviously can give very little evidence of profitability and prospects, credit-worthiness is frequently based on the bank manager's personal assessment of the applicant. The new firm has special difficulties in providing evidence, and the new firm with relatively small equity capital is in a particularly disadvantageous position because banks are reluctant to have a bigger stake in the firm than the owners themselves. One possible way for a lender to take account of special risks of this sort is to charge a higher rate of interest, but this is foreign to normal banking practice. Banks do of course charge differential rates, and give lower rates to "blue chip" customers; with present structures and conventions, however, they are unable to charge sufficient to cover many of the risks inherent in venture financing, which may realistically require differential charges of the order of 10 per cent. Even so, banks do sometimes help a new firm to set up in business if satisfied as to the integrity of the borrower and the security of the assets.

Overdrafts are also a relatively cheap form of finance; from the point of view of the borrower, bank overdrafts are particularly economical when requirements are liable to fluctuate, since interest is paid only on the debt outstanding and not on the total permitted overdraft. In addition, in many cases unused overdraft facilities represent a potential ready supply of funds which can be used before the firm has to look for outside capital.

There are several reasons why a company's overdraft may fluctuate, both from year to year and within the year. The expansion of a firm is usually discontinuous, and loans necessary during (say) a twelve-month or two-year expansion period may well become unnecessary after that particular phase of expansion is complete. Similarly, a firm may use a bank loan to buy a particular piece of machinery over a twelve-month period and not wish to buy a similar piece for several years afterwards. During the year stock requirements may fluctuate considerably and may be financed by borrowing from the bank; tax payments may account for heavy borrowing at certain times of the year; sales may fluctuate seasonally and during off-peak seasons bank overdrafts may finance the working capital of the firm. Overdrafts are also useful for tiding the entrepreneur over the occasional slight recession in his business: banks are reluctant to see their customers go bankrupt and, provided that they do not feel that they are throwing good money after bad, are usually prepared to see a firm over a bad patch.

Businesses in the Oxford Survey had variable overdrafts: of 170 businesses which had overdrafts, 121 had them in most years, but 143 had them on average for less than six months in the year.

Balance-sheet figures rarely give the bank borrowing position of a business: they only show bank credit outstanding at the balance-sheet date, and this may give a misleading impression; where the overdraft fluctuates there is no reason to suppose that the balance-sheet date will coincide with the date of borrowing. The level of bank credit outstanding at a particular date does not necessarily reflect its importance to the business: there is some reason to suspect that bank credit would be less than normal on balance-sheet date, partly because of "window-dressing," and partly because of the convenience of having a balance-sheet date when stocks, and also bank credit and possibly trade creditors, are also low. In the Oxford Survey thirty-eight out of 214 businesses which showed nil bank credits in the balance sheet had in fact borrowed from the bank during the preceding five years.

Although approximately half of the companies in the Oxford Survey did not have any bank loans at all, to those which did use them they were of considerable importance; in 10 per cent. of cases bank loans amounted to over 50 per cent. of net assets. The average for all firms (9·8 per cent.) was over twice the average for quoted public companies (4·1 per cent.); and for firms which actually had an overdraft the average was about 20 per cent. Some indication of this importance is that, whereas in *Studies in Company Finance* (see *Bib.* 82), if bank credit exceeded 10 per cent. of net assets, it was classified as "large" (in which category come about half of the public companies with overdrafts), in private companies it is more appropriate to think of 25 per cent. as representing large bank credit. Private companies make much more frequent and heavy use of bank credit than quoted public companies: only 35 per cent. of public companies surveyed in *Studies in Company Finance* (see *Bib.* 83) had overdrafts, and only 23 per cent. had overdrafts in five or six years; in the Oxford Survey the proportions were 47 and 30 per cent.

Boswell (see *Bib.* 21) also found that businesses financed by ICFC showed a much higher level of bank borrowing than quoted companies with which they were compared.

The general picture is that small, young, rapidly growing businesses rely heavily on bank credit; they tend to be rather illiquid and to be extensive users of all other forms of short- and medium-term money, including hire-purchase and trade credit. They are businesses which are hungry for funds, may have inadequate savings, but may impress the bank manager with their potential profitability. Boswell (see *Bib.* 21) also noted that, "ICFC customers tend already to have tapped bank credit to the full—otherwise they would hardly have applied for finance—and the larger part of their continuing bank borrowing does then appear to be relatively stable and continuous."

Businesses which do not use bank credit are, by contrast, older, larger and static or declining. Many owners have objections to any sort of borrowing outside the business and prefer to finance their development out of resources; this frequently takes much longer and such concerns grow slowly. Many older businesses similarly have carried out any expansion which they felt was necessary, and having had time to accumulate resources of their own, have less need of bank credit or indeed any other of the shorter- and medium-term sources of funds.

Borrowing from the bank is usually the most convenient source of funds for the small growing concern, and for most businesses the bank is the first place they look for funds. The businessman is already likely to have an account with a bank and may well be prepared to talk about his financial problems more readily to his own local bank manager than to anyone else. On the other side the local bank manager is able to assess the prospects of the business rather better than some outside organisation. And once a bank has decided to provide finance it rarely wishes to withdraw support. The bank loan is also one of the simpler forms of finance to arrange, and it is frequently cheaper than any other comparable way of borrowing. Unfortunately there is little doubt that at times of credit restraint, smaller businesses may be particularly vulnerable through their dependence on bank overdrafts.

The tendency in recent years for banks to enter into rather longer-term lending may of course upset some of these advantages. The local bank manager may not have the technical facilities at hand to enable him to assess the prospects of a middle-sized industrial project: the head office may have, but they may be disinclined to undertake a fairly extensive investigation for what is to them (if not to the borrower) a fairly small sum. And further, going to head office may cancel out the advantages of close local contact.

But these disadvantages must be weighed against the undoubted advantages that would follow on the further development of medium-term lending by the banks, and indeed one might expect an improvement in the genuine financial expertise of bankers as the competition increases and the developments gather pace. It is in this field that the banks could be of most help to small businesses and could make a major contribution to the filling of the Macmillan Gap.

Bank borrowing is the source of funds with which most business men are familiar. The main guidelines associated with it are:

(a) The bank is likely to be the first source to which the business will consciously look for funds.

(*b*) Bank borrowing is best seen as short-term and the overdraft is not for long-term capital.

(*c*) But many businesses have a certain hard core of bank borrowing which is really part of long-term debt.

(*d*) Longer-term borrowing from the bank may be possible, and is worth trying.

(*e*) The banker will want financial statements, budgets and (possibly) cash flows: the businessman should therefore go along either with such statements ready prepared or with his information from which they can be prepared.

(*f*) It is better to anticipate the need for borrowing than to ask in emergency.

(*g*) If one bank will not help, another one might, and the businessman should be prepared to look elsewhere.

CHAPTER 8

TRADE CREDIT*

CREDIT extended by businesses to each other and to customers in the normal course of business has always been one of the most important sources of funds in the economy. It is of particular significance to the small firm. Many businessmen who proudly proclaim that they never borrow are merely failing to take into account their trade credit position. Indeed it has been said that one can run a business without cash, but not without credit and debt.

Trade credit works in two directions. The firm grants credit to its customers; these appear as "debtors" or "accounts receivable" on the assets side of the balance sheet; it receives credit from its suppliers and this item appears as "trade creditors" or "accounts payable" among the liabilities on the balance sheet. Both of these items are usually large in most concerns, and indeed it would be difficult to carry on business at all without some mutual credit of this sort.

The provision of credit to customers represents the acquisition of an operating asset, which is just as necessary to the business in many respects as the fixed assets which make the goods. Like all assets, debtors need to be financed, however: to some extent they are financed by the firm receiving similar credits from suppliers but the two rarely balance; the firm which provides more credit than it receives will do so by the use of its retained profits, its overdraft or any of the other sources of finance available to it. Some firms, on the other hand, receive more credit from suppliers than they grant to customers: they are therefore net receivers of funds.

Trade credit in small and big business

Trade credit is essentially short term and, as in the case of bank credit, the amounts shown in the balance sheet give no more than a snapshot of a position at an arbitrary date. Trade creditors form a heterogeneous group, and sums other than pure trade credit and debt are often included; *e.g.* hire-purchase due, sums due for wages, rents, sums due for purchase tax, etc., are all included in creditors, and

* References to the Bibliography are indicated. *e.g.* see *Bib.* 25; the Bibliography is to be found on pages 177–181.

loans to associated concerns, if of a fairly short-term nature, are frequently included in debtors. Although giving and receiving of credit is fairly automatic in the normal course of business and is fairly constant throughout the year, a great deal is also seasonal and depends on the volume of stock purchases and sales of finished goods: such seasonality is not reflected in balance-sheet figures. Short-term flows of trade credit may well be of major significance; they cannot be observed but they must be planned.

Trade creditors, or accounts payable, form the major part of outside debt of small businesses; trade debtors, or accounts receivable, come second to stocks and work in progress in importance as current assets. In over 40 per cent. of cases in the Oxford Survey, for example, creditors and debts exceeded 50 per cent. of net assets; the average at March 31, 1954, was 23·2 per cent. for creditors and 35·3 for debtors, compared with 18·6 and 24·2 per cent. respectively in public companies. Boswell (see *Bib.* 21) also found a more important role for trade credit in private companies financed by ICFC. One explanation of the large debtors of small firms is that they may be less efficient and strict in the collection of their debts, and they are frequently in a rather weak position to ask debtors to pay quickly, particularly if the debtors are large firms.

A great deal of trade credit is granted and received in normal day-to-day business: trade credit is received when materials are bought, and granted when goods are sold: credit given fluctuates with changes in turnover of the firm, and credit received fluctuates with stocks. There is a closer relationship between increases than there is between decreases. When they are increasing their stocks firms usually take more credit from suppliers, but when reducing stocks they are less ready to reduce outstanding debt to suppliers. The difference is more marked with debtors and turnover; when turnover is increasing firms give more credit, but when sales fall, firms find it more difficult to get debtors to reduce outstanding debt, or may even have to offer better credit terms in order to sell anything at all.

For many purposes it is convenient to think of net trade credit granted or received as the significant element from the point of view of the individual business. Net trade credit is the difference between creditors and debtors: it represents net funds granted or received by the firm on this account. Although the net amount is small in relation to the total sums involved it is of great significance in small companies. Differences between private and public companies are marked; although proportionately more public companies receive net trade credit, when private companies receive trade credit the sums involved are relatively much larger. The granting and receiving of net trade credit is of much more significance to private companies and unincorporated businesses than it is to quoted public companies.

An alternative way of measuring the relative importance of creditors and debtors is the creditor–debtor ratio, frequently calculated in business in the assessment of the financial position of a company.

There are good reasons why debtors should normally exceed creditors, or in other words why net trade credit should normally be given. To some extent this difference is reduced by the predisposition of many accountants slightly to overvalue creditors and to undervalue debtors, but this still leaves wide gaps in the majority of firms. Part of the difference between the two is due to value added to materials in the process of production, and it would be expected that, the higher was value added, and the lower were material costs as a proportion of total costs, the greater would be the difference.

The type of business done by the firm also affects the size of net trade credit. In some trades, for example, manufacturers may have to pay spot cash for materials, or to pay within a short period and allow customers longer credit.

Trade credit policies and practices depend very much on the industry within which the business operates. In the clothing industry, for example, borrowing on trade credit is fairly common; this probably reflects the ease of entry stemming from low capital needs in the industry. H. B. Rose pointed out to the Radcliffe Committee (see *Bib*. 72): "In general one would expect to find the net receipt of trade credit playing an important part in the case of trades into which entry is comparatively easy, in which many businesses operate at the margin of profitability except in times of vigorous booms."

Differences between industries also reflect the relationship between the firm and its customer: businesses which work mainly on specification orders for regular customers tend to give credit; businesses which make their own products and place them on the market without advance orders tend to receive credit. This suggests that firms working on contract for other firms are very much at their mercy when it comes to receiving payment for work done. Government institutions are frequently mentioned as bad payers of trade debts.

The Oxford Survey showed great variability of the ratio of

turnover to debtors in small businesses; this is partly explained by the fact that many firms do not have any rigid ideas or policy about the proportion of sales which they finance by giving credit.

The giving of extra trade credit is sometimes a form of competition, either in the market or in tenders for contracts, but small firms are unable to offer any realistic threats in their attempt to collect debts, although they can employ debt collectors for small fees, and commonly do so in the retail trade; to some extent they may be exploited by customers who realise their semi-monopsonistic position.

To some extent debtors are financed by creditors, partly in many cases as a matter of conscious policy by the firm; the motives for the granting and receipt of credit are different, however, and the one will not consciously finance the other. Granting of credit to customers depends very much on the salesman or sales director within the limits of company policy (if any), and may be the active side of the credit business, whilst payment of bills may be virtually an automatic or at least passive, procedure with the firm, carried out either as a routine clerical procedure or in accordance with the custom of the trade. Frequently, however, a high level of output, which may mean more debtors, will involve high stocks and a correspondingly high level of creditors: the two, although differently motivated, may therefore move hand in hand.

Credit-reporting agencies exist which will provide assessments of a customer's credit-worthiness; many firms insist on trade references before they will grant trade credit; some carry out their own credit inquiries, but few small firms carry out such relatively sophisticated investigations. To the extent that they rely on one or two customers there is less possibility of allowing such knowledge to affect their credit policy; many firms complain about the slowness of settlement of debts by government departments and larger firms than themselves. A heavy load of slow-paying accounts ties up a great deal of the firm's working capital, and may well retard its growth, but how far firms are prepared to go to cure such troubles depends on individual circumstances.

Other factors, some of a financial nature, some connected with the firms' behaviour patterns, also influence trade credit and help to explain many differences in the credit structure of these firms.

Young, small, rapidly growing businesses are more likely to be large receivers of net trade credit. It is often argued that if creditors exceed debtors (*i.e.* the firm receives net trade credit) this is a sign of "over-trading," which consists of attempting the expansion of a business without adequate background of liquid capital. The danger of over-trading is that the returns from trading lag behind expenditure, and after a time creditors become restive and may in time enforce liquidation. Certainly growing firms are liable to such dangers, but the dangers only materialise if the firm is unable to finance its expenditure by other means: looking at creditors and debtors in isolation only tells part of the story, and inhibition of a virile growing firm might well result if too much attention was paid to cautious counsels based on this relationship alone.

Use of trade credit as a source of funds is closely associated with use of other sources of funds. The main danger in this situation lies in the fact that most of the borrowing of small businesses is short and medium term and this may in itself be a reflection of potential instability, often resulting as much from imperfections in the capital market as from inherent instability of the business.

Trade credit is just one further form of credit which small growing firms use in their "credit hunger."

The financing of trade credit

To some extent the receipt of credit from suppliers helps to finance the giving of credit to customers but the two rarely balance. Where firms receive more credit than they grant they are using net trade credit as an additional source of funds, and this is of considerable importance to many small firms, but many businesses give more credit than they receive. The difference between the two needs to be financed in just the same way as any other activity: to some extent the finance will come from general sources, such as retained profits and overdrafts, but there are some specialised ways of financing trade credit.

Until the nineteenth century most of this credit would have been given and received in the form of bills of exchange, the use of which dates back at least to the fourteenth century. The "inland" bill is sometimes suitable for the finance of transactions on the home market—for the purchase of materials and components, but not, as a rule, for the purchase of finished goods—but nowadays bills of exchange are rarely used on the home market and their use is largely confined to the export trade. Most businesses prefer the looser and more flexible form of book credits.

In his memorandum of evidence to the Radcliffe Committee (see *Bib.* 72), H. B. Rose reported that there had been some increase in inland bill finance in recent years, and mentioned that bills are also drawn by finance houses or commercial concerns for transactions outside their normal hire-purchase business and rediscounted with discount houses (this is probably explained largely by their familiarity with this form of financing). There is no evidence of how important domestic trade bills are in total, and it must be supposed that in most trades they are relatively unimportant, but their use may be increasing.

Banks are frequently prepared to lend against accounts receivable, and sometimes indeed regard debts as better security than goods awaiting sale. Debtors which have been covered by credit insurance are particularly good and secure assets on which funds can be raised. Rose estimated that the value of domestic business covered by credit insurance is about £1,000 million, which is a small proportion of total turnover. Such insurance is commonest in textiles, clothing, building and the timber trades, which have predominantly small firms and fluctuating markets. To the extent that an increase in debtors is evidence of growth this may also help the growing firm to obtain funds; but this must be weighed against the powerful arguments against over-trading and the attempt to grow too fast.

Rose also pointed to the ". . . growing if still small part played in recent years in the finance of non-hire-purchase credit by various finance houses." Such lenders will naturally lend only to firms with good credit-standing but, in return for a higher rate of interest, they are frequently prepared to take more risks than a bank. This is particularly true of the smaller and newer finance houses, which may, however, be more selective in the type of debts which they will handle.

The credit advanced by retailers to customers is frequently financed by hire-purchase. Hire-purchase outstanding in Britain is in the region of £1,200 million, of which approximately two-thirds is held by finance houses, the rest being owed direct to the shops. On the whole, big retailers finance part of their own hire-purchase; smaller retailers tend to have associations with finance houses, but an increasing proportion of larger retailers are relying on the specialised services of finance houses. The usual procedure is for the retailer to ask the finance house to give facilities to customers, but it is also common for the retailer to enter into a direct agreement with the customer and to sell (or "block-discount") these debts to a finance house for a proportion of their full value. As will be seen later hire-purchase is also used by small businesses for the purchase of equipment, and this points to further possibilities, from the seller's point of view, of financing trade debtors by hire-purchase.

The business should also keep a close watch on its debtors, and it may pay to induce customers, by means of substantial discounts, to pay more quickly. Neither of these is particularly easy for the small firm.

Britain, unlike the United States, has no large, well-organised market in trade credit, but certain arrangements with suppliers are possible, and these allow a firm to free some of the funds which it may have tied up in debtors or to regularise its borrowing on trade credit. In some industries, particularly the engineering trades, the "free issue materials" system is adopted; under this system the customer provides the manufacturer with materials free of charge, paying merely for the costs of manufacture. A variant of this system is for the customer to help the manufacturer with the purchase of stocks; and similarly tooling charges may be met by the customer, with appropriate safeguards. The major danger of this sort of agreement is that it may involve too close ties with suppliers or customers, with the danger of loss of independence or control.

Factoring

A form of finance which is spreading in Britain is factoring. This practice is relatively common in the United States. The principle is simple: the manufacturer sells his goods to the factor for a discount; the factor is then responsible for collecting the debts. The factor may either pay immediately, in which case the manufacturer's funds are freed for other purposes, and his liquid funds can expand as his sales grow; this is a useful way of financing increasing sales without depending on outside sources of funds; alternatively he may pay on the date when the client would settle his bills. The second method merely relieves the manufacturer of the work associated with the collection and checking of accounts, and does not result in any increase in funds available, but even this service is frequently worth while for the small firm which cannot afford a specialised service of its own. Some of the risk is also removed in this way, but in general factors are reluctant to handle risky business. The charge for the second type of service is usually in the region of 1–2 per cent. of turnover, deducted as commission by the factors; the charge for factoring proper is a substantial discount (usually in the range of 12–15 per cent. per annum).

An important feature of this sort of factoring is that it is a form of finance *without recourse*: the factor assumes all responsibility for the debt.

A variant of factoring is what is known in the United States as "accounts receivable" financing, which is a credit arrangement under which the manufacturer obtains cash on a continuing basis on the security of his debtors: the debtors are pledged to the lender, who does not take any responsibility for the soundness or for the collection of the debt. This is the sort of credit finance which hire-purchase finance houses undertake in Britain.

So far factoring of any kind has not been of very great importance in Britain, but its use is growing, particularly in the export trade and one or two specialist financial institutions have been founded. It is frequently argued that one main feature inhibiting the growth of factoring in Britain is the fear that intervention of the factor between the business and its client might affect goodwill and might suggest financial instability.

This objection can be met by "undisclosed factoring," or undisclosed non-recourse finance, a system under which the factor buys the goods from the manufacturer before delivery, and then appoints the manufacturer as agent to complete the sale and collect payment on the factor's behalf. No loss of goodwill is involved, and there is no need to duplicate the overheads of invoicing and collecting the debts; for the firm which does not posses its own special department this is not of course a major advantage. The cost of undisclosed factoring is normally over 7 per cent. per annum, but the actual charge depends on the business and the current level of Bank Rate.

All of these methods have a major advantage in common: the businessman liberates the cash tied up in debtors. This is important not only as an immediate source of funds but also because it may help to restore freedom of manoeuvre: the firm is no longer inhibited by its illiquidity in its search for other funds, or alternatively it may be able to pay its creditors more quickly and take advantage of trade discounts. In effect a company which uses factoring may well enjoy an increase in cash resources of the order of 15 per cent. of annual turnover on a continuing basis. But factoring is not necessarily an alternative to other sources of funds, and a company with a high proportion of factored debts might not be in a good position to get an overdraft.

The very small business is rarely in a position to make adequate use of factors. There are economies of scale in factoring as in any other form of business activity, and a very small turnover is rarely suitable for this form of finance. Normally the lowest level would be around £150,000 per year, but there are exceptions; for example, a well-established business with a high proportion of its trade debts outstanding to a small number of good customers might well find that a factor would take on its business even if annual turnover fell below £100,000 per year; in other circumstances a wide range of customers with short-term debts may be more attractive. This apart, most businesses which sell on terms offering credit of between one and three months are suitable, and it is usually desirable that there should be a fairly large number of customers. Examples of industries in which factoring has proved successful are: light engineering, toys, clothing, sand and gravel merchants, and meat packers, and its use is extending to other industries.

Factoring is still in its infancy in Britain, but it is growing. It is a competitive field, and the number of factoring companies in Britain is less than a dozen.

A possibility which has been barely explored in the United Kingdom is credit insurance of debts, which would make it a great deal easier for the business to liquidate its tied-up assets. Credit insurance of exports is well established, and provides an example of its value; further developments in the field however depend either on the establishment of a new institution or special co-operative arrangement between businesses.

The costs of trade credit

The dependence of small firms on trade credit is probably excessive and a sign of financial weakness, and the evidence suggests that small private companies are much more dependent on the form of credit than are the large quoted public companies. In the United States before the war there was evidence (see *Bib.* 83) that small businesses differed a great deal from big public corporations in that they relied heavily on trade credit at high cost. Although increasing prosperity since the war may have improved the financial position of many firms in the United States, there is still evidence that small firms rely more heavily on trade credit than do public corporations.

One of the dangers of excessive reliance on trade credit is the high cost. In his memorandum to the Radcliffe Committee, H. B. Rose discussed the terms of credit, and showed that there is a wide variety of practices in British industry relating in the main to the length of credit granted and discounts for prompt payment. Credit terms granted seem to depend to some extent on the traditions and customs of the trade in which the business is operating, and some trade associations have fairly strict rules about trade credit terms and discounts; but there is little doubt that on occasion the extension of trade credit on more favourable terms can be a way of extending sales.

According to Rose the most common cash discount appears to be $2\frac{1}{2}$ per cent. for one month (a period which may be extended), but there are several different practices: in building components he mentions $3\frac{3}{4}$ per cent. for seven days, $2\frac{1}{2}$ per cent. for one month; in worsted cloth 5 per cent. for seven days; in edible fats 2d. in the pound for seven days.

In some industries (steel, oil, coal and chemicals, for example) transactions between large firms carry no cash discounts, with credit periods of up to one month. This is rather an expensive form of finance, but in some cases it costs little more to take three months' credit than to take just over one month. Rose suggests reasons, other than the ignorance and inertia which may be common, why many concerns do not make more intensive efforts to qualify for discounts: firms are reluctant to reduce their own indebtedness by putting stronger pressure on debtors, because of the effect on their sales; small firms may be close to overdraft limits, and eager to use any form of credit; the taking of trade credit from suppliers is easier than borrowing from a bank or a finance house (this is not always true). He adds that in non-boom times many buyers simply deduct discount and do not make payment within the time stipulated.

Rose also points out that, ". . . the nearer one gets to transactions carried out between small businesses the less clearly defined and the more flexible do trade credit terms become. There is more adaptation to individual circumstances, including credit status, more bargaining and more competition." All of which tends to make things more difficult for the small concern.

In the United States the most frequently quoted (see *Bib.* 33) figure for discount is 2 per cent. for prompt payment within ten to fifteen days, but there is a wide variety of charges and practices, much as in the United Kingdom.

Charges are high, but they vary little with variations of interest rates in general, and indeed the Radcliffe Committee (see *Bib.* 72) concluded that the volume of trade credit is largely unaffected by interest rates. Trade credit is on the whole unlikely to be reduced by monetary policy; and indeed it introduces an extra element of elasticity into the credit structure of the economy. But it has to be financed from somewhere, and a period of general tightness of money usually means that trade credit tends to get tighter as well. During periods of credit restraint many firms react to tighter credit by taking longer credit from their suppliers, who in many cases are unable to protest effectively. Many firms try to reduce credit extended to customers by demanding prompt payment. But the extent to which this is possible depends very much on the relative bargaining strength of suppliers and customers. The retail trade certainly tries hard to reduce credit given to customers.

The dangers of excessive trade credit are fairly obvious: if a firm gives too much in pursuit of sales, as is not uncommon in the early phases of a company's life, it is in danger of overtrading and also runs the risk of acquiring bad debts; if it receives too much credit it is acquiring short-term liabilities, frequently without the current assets with which to pay them off (*i.e.* it is becoming highly illiquid). Both of these are dangers to which small firms are more prone than large firms.

The systematic control and financing of trade credit can contribute a great deal to the solution of the financial difficulties of the small firm; it is encouraging that a market for such credit is beginning to evolve in Great Britain. But it is a slow process and in this, as in many other fields, a great deal must still depend on the initiative of the businessman and the counsel of his financial advisers.

Trade credit is an area in which a great deal of money can be saved and in which funds can be raised; it is much more complex than many businessmen realise, and a financial adviser might suggest the following appreciation:

(*a*) Decide how much credit can be given (what proportion of sales, what total limit) and for how long; remember that the manufacturer and trader is not usually in business as a supplier of credit.

(*b*) Assess customers (how much credit they may be given, for how long), collect references, analyse their balance sheets and so on.

(c) What are normal trade terms, and is it desirable to change them?

(d) Establish a regular collection procedure and a procedure for overdue accounts.

(e) Bad debts, although some are inevitable, are very expensive, because the loss is of the whole cost, not merely the profit.

(f) Consider factoring.

(g) Consider credit insurance.

(h) Credit received must also be managed; it is important to avoid overtrading or at the very least to be conscious of what one is doing if accounts payable are allowed to accumulate. Liquidity is as important as solvency, but it should not be an obsession.

(i) The timing and amount of payments by customers and to suppliers are an integral part of cash-flow forecasts.

CHAPTER 9

OTHER SOURCES OF FUNDS*

DIRECTORS' LOANS

THE director's loan is a form of finance very rarely used by the
public company but frequently used by the private company, and just
over a quarter of the firms in the Oxford Survey used such loans at
one time or another in the period 1950–1956. Partners, too, make
loans to their businesses on much the same sort of basis. Such loans
by directors and partners are normally fairly small (rarely more than
£10,000) but can be very large and very important in some cases.

The director's loan is a way of borrowing from a director without
giving him an extra share in the equity of the firm; and this may be an
important reason for the use of this form of finance in private companies. Such loans are frequently temporary and the money may
merely be lent in order to tide the company over a difficult period:
such periods commonly occur in early stages of growth. In such
cases, although the amounts may be relatively small they are of great
strategic importance and may mean the difference between survival
and death of a firm. Frequently, once lent, the money remains in the
firm, in which case the director usually receives interest on it, at
approximately the same rate as on a deposit account.

A director's motives in lending in this way may be complex. It is
hardly a liquid investment in most cases, particularly in early stages
when the money has just been lent, and frequently the director could
well be earning more by placing the money elsewhere. Cases are
related of directors who simply leave the money in the form of a loan
in the hope that one day the board may decide to offer him shares in
lieu, but this must usually be a forlorn hope. A situation may well
arise, however, in which the director would threaten to remove his
loan, at great embarrassment to the firm, unless he was given a bigger
share in the equity of the firm, and greater control, in its place.

Frequently, of course, the director's loan may simply be an
accumulation of directors' fees in a special loan account, and this

* References to the Bibliography are indicated, *e.g.* see *Bib.* 25; the Bibliography is to be
found on pages 177–181.

134

may be used because of its mutual convenience to the director and the firm.

From the point of view of the firm such loans are potentially very useful. A director will rarely sabotage his interests by threatening to withdraw a loan, though he may well use the loan as a bargaining weapon in order to get his own way. Nevertheless the loans are normally short term in character (unless they are the subject of a special agreement) and are open to some of the dangers of short-term credit. In cases where directors' loans are either substantial or long term, both the business and its potential lenders may well be wise to think of them as part of the capital employed in the business, whether or not this is the formal situation; the reason for this is that if such borrowing is stable and long-lasting, it should be treated as part of long-term financial resources.

Directors' loans tend to be used mainly by those firms which are heavy users of all forms of outside short- and medium-term credit. There must be a suspicion that the director's loan is frequently used to rescue a firm in trouble: the extent to which this happens depends on how able and willing directors are to help in this way.

Bank managers tend to be suspicious of large directors' loans in the balance sheet, fearing that the item may be merely a form of window-dressing undertaken in order to give a false impression of the financial position of the firm, and knowing that this form of finance may be easily withdrawn. Suspicion would be heightened in cases where the loan only appeared in the balance sheet a short time before a request for bank advance was made; it is at least possible that a director may borrow on short term in order to lend to the firm for this purpose, and banks are alive to this possibility.

Loans from private individuals are similar to loans from directors, and may well be arranged in certain circumstances; but their availability depends very much on personal contact and knowledge. Such loans may occasionally be given on condition that the lender becomes a director. Loans from individuals are in fact rare in small firms, and it must be doubted whether they are a significant form of finance in general.

Hire-Purchase

Hire-purchase is a form of medium-term credit which has come into increasing use in business in recent years; it is fairly commonly used for the purchase of industrial plant, and it is also being used more and widely in the distributive trades. Big companies rarely buy in this way, but hire-purchase is frequently used by small businesses for relatively small purchases of machinery and motor vehicles. A quarter of the firms in the Oxford Survey used this method of finance, typically for goods in two price ranges, one around £750, the other in the region of £5,500; the average debt was over £1,000, and for those firms which used hire-purchase it accounted for about 6 per cent. of current liabilities.

Hire-purchase is mainly used by small, rapidly growing firms at an early stage of their development. It is particularly useful because it is one of the ways in which a new business may become established and survive the difficult initial stages of setting up and growth. As the firm grows and as its financial strength improves its need for such methods is less, and bigger companies rarely use hire-purchase.

This form of finance is particularly convenient in cases where machines and plant have to be bought in fairly large, indivisible units; this is the kind of plant which the new concern frequently needs on setting up, and which the growing firm needs when it is expanding. But hire-purchase is less commonly used for replacements of machinery, although vehicles may be replaced in this way, largely because most firms make provision for replacement from their profits.

Hire-purchase is used by firms in all industries, and particularly in industries, such as clothing, printing and light engineering, which use plant of a type which lends itself particularly to this form of finance; sewing machines, printing machines and lathes are common examples. And most small firms need some sort of transport for their goods and cars for managers and salesmen; the motor-vehicle field is one which is traditionally associated with hire-purchase. But as well as being used by manufacturing concerns it is commonly used by motor traders, car-hire firms, transport and coach undertakings, farmers, contractors, garage proprietors, retailers and caterers; and it is rare to find a trade in which hire-purchase is not used.

Hire-purchase has several advantages for the small firm. From the borrower's point of view it is fairly easy to arrange and, although this may seem illogical, many businessmen prefer to borrow in this fairly routine, impersonal way than to go cap in hand to the bank manager and have to explain or defend the request. This does not mean that hire-purchase finance companies do not want to know about a firm's affairs, and the first transaction always involves some inquiries into credit status, although later transactions may well be rather easier. A business hire-purchase agreement is similar in principle to that between a private consumer and a finance company: the buyer asks the finance company to buy the asset, hires it for a specified period and then exercises the option to buy it for a nominal sum when all hire charges and instalments have been paid. So long as the instalments are kept up, the hirer has free right to use of the goods as though they were his own.

But the actual transaction is usually more complex than that involved in buying a piece of furniture. The intending purchaser not only needs to give details of the things he wishes to buy; he must also be prepared to give other information, usually including data from his accounts, and perhaps an explanation of what the goods are to be used for. Bearing these and similar matters in mind the finance house will then offer terms for the transaction, specifying deposit required, period of repayment, number and amount of instalments, and hire-purchase charges.

A major advantage is that there is usually no need to provide security in the usual form, since no actual loan is provided, and the ownership of the goods by the finance house is security in itself. There are complications, of course, and there may be cases where the goods disappear in the act of production, or are not repossessable for one reason or another, or have little value outside their current use; but, as will be seen, such goods are not ideally suited to hire-purchase and can rarely be financed in this way. It is clear, too, that the finance company has a right to expect certain conditions to be observed, and most agreements oblige the hirer to maintain the asset in good order, insure it, and also not to sell it without the consent of the finance company (the last is in any case illegal). These requirements are usually sufficient, but there are occasions when additional security may be asked for, in the form of guarantees from directors or private individuals.

From the point of view of the finance house there is one special difficulty of hire-purchase credit advanced to business concerns. Much industrial equipment is specific to certain tasks and may have little value outside the firm which buys and uses it. It therefore represents inadequate security and, where re-sale value is not closely related to purchase price, some further security may well be needed.

But many finance houses will take this risk if they are convinced that on other grounds the purchaser is credit-worthy.

The Finance Houses Association offers general guidance on the type of goods most suitable for hire-purchase financing in industry and commerce:

"(1) it should be possible to identify the goods readily; they should not, for example, consist of a number of component parts of a larger piece of equipment, or large numbers of small unidentifiable items;

"(2) the goods should command a reasonably free re-sale market and should at all times have a market value greater than the amount currently owed under the hire-purchase agreement;

"(3) the goods should be durable and have a useful life greater than the period of the hire-purchase agreement;

"(4) the goods should have a high-earning potential from the beginning of their useful life so that they can earn sufficient to pay off the hire-purchase debt over the period of the agreement; a few examples of high-earning assets suitable for hire-purchase financing are: earth-moving machinery, road haulage vehicles, motor coaches, machine tools, printing machinery, plastic moulding machinery."

In the same way as banks, the reputable finance companies are usually reluctant to cause their clients extra embarrassment by withdrawing support, and they are not anxious to repossess goods in the event of failure to pay instalments, unless all else fails. They will frequently accommodate the hirer, perhaps by extending the period of the agreement, provided that they see a reasonable chance of being paid. But, if the agreement is broken, the hire-purchase company can, if it so wishes, repossess the goods.

But finance houses are not charitable institutions and are not merely last-resort sources of funds; they will, in other words, look just as closely at an application for funds as will any financial institution. Like many other lenders, they find problems when assessing loan applications from small firms, and are inclined to look askance at such traditional problems as lack of equity capital, excessive loan capital from proprietors, lack of unencumbered security, over-trading and lack of experience and continuity of management. Hire-purchase is not an easy way out.

Many firms are like private consumers in that they are not

prepared to liquidate assets when an alternative easy source is at hand; many of the firms in the Oxford Survey were however illiquid and the evidence suggests that many which bought goods on hire-purchase did not in fact have such assets which they could liquidate, and used this form of finance as one of the many sources which they needed.

Hire-purchase is also rather longer-term than many comparable forms of finance; three to five years is nowadays the most common repayment period for industrial agreements, but government restrictions may from time to time require a shorter period. It also represents a fairly easy repayment burden for an earning asset, and since the firm also knows its commitments it can budget for them (but a well-organised firm does this in any case).

It is sometimes argued that by using hire-purchase a firm leaves other lines of finance for emergency; this is a doubtful proposition. If a firm waits until it is in serious trouble before it applies for a bank loan or help from an institution it is most unlikely to get such funds, and hire-purchase itself is much better used (if it can be obtained) in an emergency than bank borrowing. It does, however, allow the firm to economise its cash and to use other credit facilities for the purchase of materials, etc.

There are disadvantages, however. Hire-purchase is not cheap and charges are much higher than market rates of interest (15–20 per cent. on a reducing balance is not uncommon); but charges fluctuate less than interest rates because interest is only a small proportion of the total charge. Many businessmen feel, however, that the difference between hire-purchase charges and interest rates are small, and in any case the expenses are allowable against tax. And usually the earning capacity of the equipment is expected to be more than sufficient to bear the burden of charges, which are, moreover, only incurred for a relatively short period. The higher are general interest rates the more attractive is hire-purchase. And during periods of credit restraint when hire-purchase has usually been less controlled in total than other forms of credit, hire-purchase is often used as an alternative to less easily accessible sources of funds. Against the advantages of immediate availability of equipment without inconvenience, many businessmen feel that such disadvantages are slight.

But its very ease and convenience point to one danger of hire-purchase: there may be a temptation to use this form of finance for expenditure which may not be justified, and this is one very good reason why finance companies closely scrutinise applications. In addition, its relatively high cost does perhaps provide further evidence to support the claim that small firms pay too much for their funds.

Other things being equal, many firms would still prefer an overdraft on cost grounds, particularly if they have an established connection with a bank; for certain purposes, however, despite the extra cost, hire-purchase is a useful and acceptable alternative. As a bridge between short- and long-term funds, and as a way of filling the gap between external and internal funds the value of hire-purchase is considerable.

In recent years there has been a growing awareness of opportunities in this field. During the 1960s hire-purchase of industrial equipment more than doubled, but for several years the increase in business uses did not keep pace with the boom in consumer hire-purchase (a great deal of the large increase in hire-purchase in the late 1950s was in new and second-hand private cars and consumer durables). In December 1969, according to statistics published by the Finance Houses Association in their journal, *Credit*, industrial and building plant and equipment accounted for 13·3 per cent. of new instalment credit extended by finance houses; at the end of December 1969 this category of commodity accounted for 14·8 per cent. of all credit outstanding to finance houses.

Imperfect knowledge of opportunities for this form of credit on the part of buyers and sellers for many years restricted the volume of business hire-purchase; it is much more widely known nowadays. The situation is similar to that in the field of consumer goods, where, for example, many second-hand deals between private individuals fall through because of a lack of knowledge of facilities. Industrialists, suppliers and their financial advisers could do a great deal themselves.

It is interesting that nowadays, notably since the entry of the banks into hire-purchase, bank managers are increasingly recommending that certain needs of small firms are best met by hire-purchase. It is not uncommon for the businessman to be advised by his bank manager to finance a proportion of his needs in the form of an overdraft and the rest by hire-purchase.

Many businessmen dislike hire-purchase: the stigma of "never-never" still dies hard despite its increasing respectability, and many feel that there is something disreputable about the whole business. This sort of objection is illogical in itself: borrowing in one form or another is frequently an essential part of the healthy growth of a business, and hire-purchase is merely a specialised form of borrowing.

In view of the financial problems of many small firms hire-purchase offers several advantages, and it is a convenient source of medium-term finance for the small and growing firm.

EQUIPMENT LEASING

There have been developments in other directions in recent years: one of the most notable of these is the growth of the practice of equipment leasing, which is similar in some respects to hire-purchase.

Hiring and leasing of plant are not new in industry: motor vehicles are frequently hired, and some specialised items of plant, such as shoemaking machinery, some office equipment, bowling alley mechanisms, etc., have long been leased; it is only in recent years however that leasing has spread on any scale to other fields. Almost any kind of equipment can nowadays be leased.

The advantages to users are fairly clear, and the method has several benefits in common with hire-purchase. Budgeting is relatively easy because commitments are known in advance, and it is also easier in many firms to fit a leasing rental into a departmental budget than it is to buy a new machine. Capital is economised, working capital is freed, and the bank overdraft and other shorter-term sources are left for normal operating needs. The problems of obsolescence are minimised (indeed they are the responsibility of the supplier), so are the heavy maintenance costs associated with the old machinery which may be the only practical alternative. No balance-sheet entry is required: this is not important itself but it may well please those who are more attached to the form of things than to their reality. In addition the whole cost of leasing can be charged against tax but, since the leasing company owns the equipment the lessee cannot charge wear and tear allowances; in the case of hire-purchase the charges only are allowable, plus depreciation on the paid-off part of the equipment.

Renting of plant is similar to leasing save that leasing is usually for a specified period, which may well be effectively the working life of the equipment, whereas a rental agreement may be for any period, which need not necessarily be specified in advance. Lease periods are usually up to five years, depending on the type of equipment and the uses to which it will be put; when the lease expires the lessee may either continue the rental, usually at a reduced rate, or abandon it and return the equipment.

The formalities of a lease are not vastly dissimilar from those of a hire-purchase transaction, with the exception that ownership does not change hands. The firm wanting the equipment usually asks the leasing company to buy it and lease it to the firm; details therefore have to be given to the leasing company, which then advises the customer of the terms which will be offered. Some credit information is frequently required and, in the case of big transactions, the leasing company may want to examine the audited accounts of the firm. In some cases additional security may be needed, perhaps in the form of guarantees from directors or private individuals. Leasing companies are, in other words, just like any other suppliers of funds in that they do not finance propositions without a careful assessment of them.

Some manufacturers of equipment do lease their own equipment, but usually the business of leasing is undertaken by specialised concerns, mainly the finance houses who also finance hire-purchase. It is usually the bigger finance houses which offer facilities, and half of the members of the Finance Houses Association and their associates undertake this sort of business.

The decision to lease depends on the assessment of the advantages of leasing, in particular of capital economy, and the possibilities of earning profit, against the disadvantages of not owning the machinery, which are not very serious, and of committing the firm to regular payments for a definite period.

Leasing requires just as careful an assessment and decision as does the financing of any capital outlay. Most accounting textbooks provide standard calculations for the lease-or-buy decision; they are essentially based nowadays on similar criteria to the discounted cash-flow approach to capital expenditure appraisal. Assuming that rates of return are the same whether the equipment is bought or leased, the question to answer is whether the net cash outflow is smaller for buying or for leasing.

In jargon terms both hire-purchase and leasing are worth while if the equipment purchased is expected to produce a cash flow which will fund the development in a period of about five years. But, whilst individual items may all be worth leasing or buying on hire purchase, if they are not seen against the background of the whole financial set up of the business, it may be tempting to take on commitments which are too heavy overall.

BILLS OF EXCHANGE

In law a bill of exchange is: "an unconditional order in writing addressed by one person to another, signed by the person giving it, requiring the person to whom it is addressed to pay on demand or at a fixed or determinable future time a certain sum in money to or to the order of a specific person or to bearer" (Bills of Exchange Act 1882).

It is most common for such bills to be payable on a fixed date; this is known as a term bill. When such a bill is presented to the drawee (the person to whom it is addressed), he acknowledges it, or "accepts" it, by signing on the face of it; the bill is then an unconditional obligation of the acceptor to pay, and what the acceptor has done in fact is to substitute his credit for that of the person drawing the bill. The system depends on the fact that the acceptor is a person or institution known to have the funds to meet the bill, even though little may be known about the drawer; and bills therefore become instruments of credit, of a known or determinable value, which may be freely bought and sold.

The use of ordinary trade bills (*i.e.* bills drawn by one trader on another) is not common in the home market, largely because individual business concerns are not usually widely known as creditworthy, and the bills are therefore not easily marketable without fairly complicated arrangements such as the taking up of banker's references. For this reason too, the rate of discount of such bills may well be high.

A much commoner form is the acceptance credit, which is a bill that has been accepted by some recognised financial institution. These are known as "bank bills." Some of these are accepted by joint stock banks; most are accepted by merchant banks, of which a small group have made the accepting of bills a large part of their business. These are known as accepting houses, and seventeen of these are members of the Accepting Houses Committee, membership of which requires two principal qualifications: the first is that a substantial part of the house's business must consist of accepting bills to finance the trade of others, the second is that its acceptances must command the finest rates in the market and be accepted by the Bank of England as "eligible paper." The Radcliffe Committee estimated that the acceptance of these houses accounted for between 20 and 25 per cent. of all bills outstanding, and for rather under half of all bank bills.

The majority of bills are employed in the overseas trade: an importer requiring finance to buy materials from abroad may draw a bill on an accepting house for the amount of the shipment; an exporter would draw a bill on an accepting house for the amount of his sales.

The method is fairly simple: the person requiring funds approaches the accepting house which, if it is satisfied as to the security, etc., issues a letter of credit to the borrower, permitting him to draw bills on the accepting house. By accepting these bills the accepting house assumes responsibility for redeeming them at maturity, and the transaction usually requires that the borrower repays the accepting house in time for it to do so. A variety of methods and conditions is possible, and a simple example will suffice. A purchaser wanting to import materials asks an accepting house to open a letter of credit in favour of the foreign shipper from whom he wishes to buy; the letter of credit will contain an undertaking to accept the bill provided that it is drawn within a stated period and accompanied by approved shipping documents giving title to the goods. The foreign shipper negotiates the bill locally, usually with his bank, and thus obtains cash for his goods on shipment; his bank sends the bill via its correspondent in London to the accepting house. The accepting house accepts the bill and returns it to the presenter, receiving in return the shipping documents, which it then provides to the original customer.

If the bill is a "sight bill," payment is made by the accepting house on receipt of the bill. If the bill is a "term bill," usually payable three months after drawing, the holder of it (in the example above, the London correspondent of the foreign bank) has a "promise to pay" of an accepting house, which he can either keep to maturity or discount with a bank or discount house. Such a bill can always be readily sold at a discount, or it can be pledged as security for an advance, and from the point of view of the holder it represents a first-class, safe, highly liquid investment. For the borrower this is a cheap and highly efficient way of obtaining short-term commercial credit.

There has been an increase in recent years in the financing of domestic trade by bills, and hire-purchase finance companies frequently finance part of their business in this way. A supplier of raw materials may grant credit to a manufacturer and draw a bill on an accepting house for the amount of the sales invoice (after providing evidence of the sale); the supplier would then receive cash from the proceeds of discounting with which to replenish his stocks. Normally the terms of the letter of credit would require him to provide the accepting house with cash to meet the bill in time for its maturity (by which time he would normally have received payment from the manufacturer). An alternative arrangement would be for the manufacturer himself to draw a bill on an accepting house to the value of his purchases, paying the supplier with the proceeds of discounting (and possibly) thereby taking advantage of a trade discount for prompt payment). When the bill reaches maturity, the manufacturer would expect to have sold the finished goods, from the proceeds of which he would pay the accepting house. Seasonal trades, too, may well finance their purchases and sales by means of acceptance credits.

It is possible to continue to use the facilities of the accepting house for more than one transaction and for extended periods by a revolving credit arrangement, which allows the borrower to draw bills as required up to an agreed limit.

The principles on which such finance are granted are simple in essence; the accepting house must be satisfied that there is an underlying commercial transaction, such as the purchase of materials or the sale of goods; and the transaction must be self-liquidating in the sense that when the bill matures, the goods financed by it should have been sold so that the proceeds are available to cover the bill. Security is usually required, although borrowers of high standing may obtain unsecured facilities; such security may be in the form of the goods purchased, which are then pledged to the accepting house, or in the form of the appropriate shipping documents; or collateral security may be required, such as Stock Exchange securities or other assets.

The cost of this form of finance depends largely on the financial standing of the borrower and the security provided. The accepting house charges a commission, which is partly a service charge for work done, and partly a remuneration for the risks inherent in giving an unconditional undertaking to pay the bills at maturity whether the borrower pays or not. To this must be added stamp duty (only 2*d*. per bill and due to disappear in any case, and the current discount rate for first-class bills; the discount rate fluctuates and is closely geared to Bank Rate, being usually between $\frac{1}{2}$ and $1\frac{1}{2}$ per cent. below Bank Rate. Thus, if acceptance commission was $2\frac{1}{2}$ per cent. per annum, and Bank Rate was 4 per cent., a typical bill of exchange would probably cost between £5 15s. and £6. Acceptance commissions range from $1\frac{1}{4}$ per cent. for more credit-worthy customers; up to 3 per cent. for other borrowers.

This means, of course, that finance by bills may well be a worthwhile alternative or additional source to borrowing by bank overdraft. Whether or not it can be used by the individual firm depends very much on custom: some trades are rarely financed in this way (it is unusual, for example, to find that bills are used in the engineering industry), and in such cases it would not be easy to borrow in this way; in other trades, however, notably those using primary commodities such as tobacco, tea, wool, timber, etc., bill finance is not uncommon.

The small firm operating mainly in the home market may well be at a disadvantage. If its trade was not customarily financed in this way, it would be unlikely that a small firm could start a new trend; and even in trades where such finance is common the small firm may well find it difficult to provide the necessary security. It is always likely that more security would be required from the small firm, and, since the accepting house would usually treat the small firm as a worse risk than a big one, the acceptance commission might well be too high for the firm to pay. But the bill of exchange is one way of financing short-term trade credit, particularly useful to the exporter or importer, but also in certain circumstances useful to the firm engaged wholly in inland trade. Bill finance is one area in which some improvements might be made which would be of some assistance to the smaller business.

THE MERCHANT BANKS

The members of the Accepting Houses Committee are the largest and most important of what are loosely called the merchant banks, a group of financial institutions which perform a wide variety of functions. Originally many of these institutions were primarily merchants, engaged in the buying and selling of goods in home and overseas trade; but as time has passed they have added a wide variety of financial activities and services. Their main function is that of an accepting house, but they have several others. Some accept deposits from the public, usually on different terms from the joint-stock banks; some grant overdraft facilities on very much the same principles as joint-stock banks; and in general many of the merchant banks act much as traditional bankers for customers, operating current accounts where desired. They may also make investments in private companies in the form of debentures and share capital, usually with a view to obtaining a quotation; and many are also issuing houses and members of the Issuing Houses Association. In this connection, too, they frequently act as advisers in problems arising from the payment of death duties (Charterhouse Industrial Development Co. is a subsidiary of one of the merchant banks); they undertake registration work and similar tasks for public companies; and many specialise in the management of unit trusts, investment trusts and private investment funds and pension and superannuation funds. Several are members of the foreign exchange and bullion markets. Some of the recent developments in factoring of receivables are due to merchant banks, and this is an aspect of their business which may well increase in time and may reinforce their accepting business; and in a related field, some merchant banks arrange for the finance of the export of capital goods.

Many of these services are of little interest to small firms, but for the expanding concern an association with a merchant bank might well have advantages as growth proceeds. This is particularly likely to be true the nearer such a firm is to the stage where transformation to public company status is being considered. As with all financial institutions, the sounder the prospects of the firm the more likely is the merchant bank to be of some help.

FINANCE FOR INNOVATIONS

The problem of small innovators was one to which the Radcliffe Committee (see *Bib.* 72) gave particular attention:

"There are certain special problems about the provision of finance for the commercial development by small businesses and private companies of new inventions and innovations of technique. One problem is that the amount of capital required to finance a development may be larger in relation to a small company's capital structure and apparent earnings prospects than the financial institutions would ordinarily feel justified in putting up."

The problem of financing innovations may be summed up briefly as that of reconciling the risks of innovation with the long period of development and the subsequent wait for rewards, which may never accrue, or may accrue to someone other than the innovator himself. The main rewards for innovations come from marketing and arise as a result of being first in the field; but the main risks arise in the development stage, when a great deal of work has to be done with little concrete prospect of reward; and the main problem of the small innovator is that of bridging the gap between the invention of a product or process and its commercial exploitation. The experience of the National Research Development Corporation is that three years is not an untypical lapse between the patenting of a process and the receipt of that first income from it.

In the large concern the problem is fairly easily catered for. There are economies of scale in research as in most business activities: most big firms have specialised research facilities whose cost is justified by the scale of operation of the firm; the risks of innovation can be absorbed as part of overhead cost and all parts of the business can contribute to the sharing of risk; the bigger the number of projects undertaken the more chance is there that some of them will turn out to be winners; by-products can be utilised; and, what is particularly important, the big firm can usually exploit the innovation itself. A survey in the United States (see *Bib.* 64) demonstrated the advantages of larger firms: only 8 per cent. of manufacturing companies with less than 100 employees had research programmes, compared with 94 per cent. of companies with over 5,000 employees. We are not so research conscious in Britain, and the differences between small and big businesses are probably even greater.

Two features of manufacturing industry in the post-war period have been the rapidity of technological change and the increasing emphasis placed by business on new product development; for the small business which wishes to survive, attention to these features is an essential part of managerial planning. The small firms can still play an important part: they can frequently concentrate on developments ignored, either deliberately or accidentally, by large concerns; they can carry out minor modifications, develop designs, etc.; and in particular they are frequently well placed to develop innovations which require ingenuity rather than large-scale resources. Many innovations stem from small firms in the engineering industry, for example, which are due to close knowledge of and deep thinking about particular specialised engineering problems.

Even so, the innovator working on a small scale frequently lacks both the commercial experience and the funds to make his innovation a success. Apart from the major risk of failure there are the other risks of innovation, high-lighted in the Radcliffe Report (see *Bib.* 72):

"... the risks in the commercial exploitation of technical innovation are likely to be greater than those in expanding an existing line of production or extending into existing lines of business; and, however promising the innovation, the risks are certainly more difficult to assess. This makes it more difficult for the company that wants to develop an invention to convince potential lenders that their money will be well invested."

The problem is largely financial, and, although in theory the small innovator has two courses open to him—to develop and manufacture for himself, or to sell his rights and patents—he all too often has to choose the latter course. And the innovator who sells his rights usually comes off badly compared with those who reap the ultimate substantial rewards: commercial history abounds with examples.

But the manufacture and marketing of an innovation may well be beyond the resources of the small innovator; and it was to help to meet this problem that the National Research Development Corporation was founded in 1948. Many innovations originate outside industry (in universities, government departments, sheds in backyards, etc.), and NRDC was set up to help in the development of these innovations in particular. The Corporation has fairly small resources and in the long run it is expected to pay its way.

NRDC gives assistance in various ways. Inventions are communicated to NRDC, which screens them and, if selected, the invention is assigned for exploitation; the rights are transferred to the Corporation, arrangements being made for the inventor to share in the revenue, and the Corporation seeks a licensee for the invention. Many of the assigned inventions are virtually ready for licensing, but many more require further technical development, which is financed by NRDC. About a third of assigned inventions are licensed; about 9 per cent. of inventions assigned have started to earn revenue; it is estimated that only about 5 per cent. of inventions communicated are likely to yield a royalty, and even that estimate is optimistic. Innovations are an inherently risky business but the Corporation has pursued a policy of accepting for assignment any invention which has reasonable prospects. Licensing is a useful function, and the resources of NRDC are helpful to the small innovator who has little experience of the exploitation of inventions. No finance is raised directly by this means, but the development of the project is financed by someone else whilst the inventor's rights are protected.

For projects which require further development NRDC is prepared to put up direct finance, but will usually do so only if industry is not prepared to develop the project on its own. NRDC very rarely shares in the equity of a firm manufacturing a product, and expects to get most of its reward from royalty payments. The Corporation will not usually undertake to help in the financing of a project which is not expected to be a commercial success, although where the national interest is clearly involved funds may be provided even where the project is fairly speculative. Not surprisingly, NRDC has preferred to concentrate its support for development projects on major rather than minor advances but is prepared to look at smaller projects. A large proportion of the innovations which come to the fore every year fall outside the scope of the Corporation: some small firms have been helped, but a good many more have not. It has been suggested that the scope of NRDC could be enlarged so that it can take a larger part in financing the innovations of small firms; many small innovators feel however, rightly or wrongly, that the NRDC approach is too restrictive for them.

The problem remains of the small innovator who develops a product or a process which appears to show some reasonable prospect of commercial success, but who requires finance. In the past these firms have had to rely on the normal channels of the market, which are not only frequently inadequate for the small firm in any case but are also inappropriate to financing innovations. Pioneer investment is outside the scope of the normal financial markets and private individuals and institutional investors do not usually feel justified in accepting the greater risks of this type of business.

Following up the recommendations of the Radcliffe Committee a new company, Technical Development Capital Ltd. (TDC), was founded in 1962, with the specific aim of providing risk capital for technical innovations and inventions. TDC is privately financed by a group of institutional investors and is modelled largely on the American Research and Development Corporation; its declared purpose is "to assist the inventor or promoters of a worthwhile development or innovation, which has passed the initial research stage but is not yet being produced commercially, to obtain the necessary capital for this purpose and to get the product on to the market." Basic research falls outside the normal province of TDC, but any projects which offer reasonable commercial possibilities are considered. "The processes of development may be long and costly, but in successful cases the rewards could be substantial." A fairly detailed investigation is conducted into the scientific and technical angles and also into financial requirements and market possibilities.

TDC sees itself operating between two existing sets of institutions: government sponsored research organisations, which do not usually finance the commercial stages of development; and institutions such as ICFC, which provide capital for established small firms but do not normally finance new ventures. Normally TDC expects to take a share in the equity of the firm, and the introductory brochure states that ". . . whatever the precise arrangements, the financial interests of the promoter will be safeguarded so that he may reap a fair reward for his enterprise." Since TDC aims to bring inventions to the stage of commercial profitability and viability, it may expect to withdraw at an appropriate time, either by sale of its interest or by making arrangements for an issue of shares.

TDC is actively concerned in looking to back good technologically based innovations; it is not a subsidy giving organisation, and it must operate on a commercial basis, but it is prepared to make its contribution to filling this particular gap by looking beyond normal criteria for the financing of a going business.

The Radcliffe Report's comment on the special problems of the innovator has led to this shortfall in the finance of innovations being referred to as the "Radcliffe Gap." The Report did not propose indiscriminate financial help for small inventors, but it did propose that an Industrial Guarantees Corporation might be set up, which would not lend directly, nor give guarantees direct, but would provide guarantees to financial institutions who themselves put up the money; technical advice could be given by the Corporation and perhaps also by NRDC. Two major merits were claimed for this approach: a manufacturer would be able to approach a wide variety of institutions, some of which would be familiar with his capabilities; and, by limiting potential losses the Corporation might induce financial institutions to adopt a more venturesome attitude to the financing of innovations. Even with TDC and other institutions which have grown up in this field, there is still likely to be a need for finance for the early stages of innovations and for research.

An interesting sidelight on the problems of innovations and the small firm is thrown by Oxford Survey data. Fifty-nine per cent. of firms in the Survey claimed that there had been no major innovations in their industry since the Second World War: four-fifths of the firms had used innovations when they knew of them, but smaller firms were less likely to use innovations (51 per cent. of firms with over 200 employees used innovations, only 24 per cent. of firms with ten to nineteen employees had used them).

Innovations are an important field. The tendency nowadays is to concentrate on technological innovation, and the development of so-called technological forecasting has focused attention on needs in this direction; the problem is receiving much more serious attention than it did. In the field of innovation as in all financial fields, however, blind faith and hope are poor substitutes for financial planning and in this particularly risky field such planning although (or perhaps because) it is more difficult, it is all the more essential. Many innovations come from people without commercial experience, and advice on feasibility and financial problems may be the service which they most need.

THE FINANCE OF EXPORTS

Exports are frequently depicted as the life-blood of the British economy, and they may well present highly profitable opportunities. But they also present difficulties, and although these are common to both large and small firms, the bigger the concern the more likely it is to have the resources for specialised departments in exports as in all other fields. Many of the problems of exporting are not financial but are specialised problems of marketing and particular exporting know how. The small business can get a great deal of help in this field from the Board of Trade (whose booklets, *Services for British Exporters*, are invaluable).

Finance does, however, present a particular problem: in addition to the general problem of financing the manufacture of goods and getting them to the buyer, the firm may also have to be prepared for the fact that the buyer may well require extended credit, and indeed for many contracts the award may well depend on the ability of the supplier to find long-term credit for the customer. There may also be more risks attached to export markets; these include, beyond the normal risks of credit-worthiness, outside influences such as war, unrest and the imposition of exchange restrictions. Thus, although the normal channels of finance are just as relevant to the finance of exports as to the finance of any other business activity, there are additional complications.

A great deal of the credit required is likely to be short term, and in the majority of cases the first approach made by the entrepreneur is to his own bank manager. In recent years the joint-stock banks in Britain have been asked by the Government to give preference to export business in making their loans and, although they are frequently deterred by the greater risks involved, they do make a significant contribution to export finance. And, even if they do not actually lend, they are usually in a position to give advice on prospects and on many of the complex technical details of exporting. It may well be in the best interests both of the bank and the businessman to raise funds by a bill of exchange, in which case introduction to a merchant bank or a confirming house, which acts for the overseas buyer is frequently made by the bank. Banks will normally require the backing of a guarantee from the Export Credits Guarantee Department.

Technical details apart, the main feature which distinguishes export business from ordinary business in the field of short-term finance is the greater risk, and the major need of many exporters is to insure against these risks. Physical risks are usually looked after in the normal way; credit risks are a different matter, and they may arise through the default of the buyer, through exchange rate variations, exchange controls, or through any of a host of economic and political risks. Some private credit-insurance concerns will insure the commercial risks of export credit, but the number is small, and the problem of export credit insurance is so vast that it can only really be tackled by a government agency.

The Export Credits Guarantee Department is a government department formed in the period between the two world wars, responsible to the President of the Board of Trade, which provides credit insurance for British exporters. It is expected to be self-supporting, and its function is not to subsidise exports. For this reason the ECGD insists on the right to insure good risks as well as bad and refuses, with certain exceptions, to insure only the most risky parts of a firm's export business. Equally, ECGD does not exist in order to provide finance for exports: its contribution to export financing is in the removal of one of the major obstacles to finance in the form of risk. ECGD lists the principal risks covered by its policies:

"Insolvency of the buyer.

"Buyer's failure to pay within six months of due date for goods which he has accepted.

"Buyer's default on contract after shipment (where not caused or excused by exporter's actions) and, where the buyer is a government, such default before shipment.

"Government action which blocks or delays transfer of payment in sterling to the exporter.

"Imposition of new import licensing restrictions in the buyer's country, or cancellation of a valid import licence.

"War between the buyer's country and Britain.

"War, revolution, or civil disturbance in the buyer's country.

"Cancellation or non-renewal of a British export licence, or imposition of new export licensing restrictions.

"Additional handling, transport, or insurance charges arising from interruption or diversion of voyage which cannot be recovered from the buyer.

"Any other cause of loss occurring outside the U.K. and not within the control of the exporter or the buyer, and not normally insurable with commercial insurers."

The exporter himself is usually required to take some share of the risk in order to ensure that he exercises "normal business prudence"; and for this reason the extent of the cover is normally restricted to 85 per cent. of loss through insolvency or protracted delay in payment, to 90 per cent. of loss through any other causes arising before shipment and, with certain exceptions, to 95 per cent. of loss where the cause arises after shipment of the goods.

Most of the business of ECGD is done under "comprehensive guarantees," usually in respect of goods sold on credit terms of up to six months: under such a policy the exporter insures the whole of his trade for a specified period. This sort of insurance is not suitable for capital projects or the export of capital goods, where contracts may be large and long term and may require extended credit: for this sort of business ECGD offers "specific policies." The period for which credit is insured depends largely on the goods sold, and ranges from about six months for consumer goods to five years for capital goods.

ECGD also offers bank guarantees which are usually restricted to individual contracts over £100,000 (for which normal "specific" or "comprehensive" policies are held). Such guarantees are given by ECGD directly to the bank discounting bills of exchange or promissory notes (or holding them as collateral), undertaking to make good default. Bank guarantees of this type are usually outside the range of business conducted by the small firm, as are the export finance guarantees designed to cover longer-term credit.

The "small exporter" scheme is available to any firm whose export turnover is less than £10,000 per year: this enables the exporter to escape the normal requirement that he has to insure a wide spread of his business with ECGD, and allows him to insure any individual buyer. A flat rate of premium is charged of 11s. 6d. for every £100 insured on any terms of credit up to 180 days; the cover is for 90 per cent. of any loss through insolvency of buyer, failure of buyer to pay at due date, and any other cause beyond the control of the exporter or the buyer arising from events outside the United Kingdom. Normal terms vary a great deal (depending on the credit-worthiness of the buyer and his country), length of credit and type of goods but under short-term policies the premium averages slightly under $\frac{1}{2}$ per cent. of the price of the goods (about 39p per £100 insured); for five-year instalment credit it may range from 3 to 10 per cent. of the price. The system is fairly easy to work: the exporter pays in advance for a "block" of cover to suit his requirements; as he insures business ECGD keeps his "credit" account, telling him when it runs out. As part of this service ECGD will also investigate credit-worthiness of buyers who are to be covered, and will furnish evidence that a particular transaction is insured. This may well place the exporter in a favourable position for obtaining bank finance for the transaction.

The "small exporter" scheme is only available for the first £20,000 of insured export business, and for two years from the date of issue; it is really intended as an introduction to ECGD and may be helpful to the small firm wishing to enter the export field for the first time.

ECGD does not provide finance direct, therefore, but it may well help in the raising of funds and it may provide the conditions under which it will be possible to raise finance. The fact that exports are insured provides a guarantee to the lender of funds that funds will be forthcoming as a result of the transaction, provided that the exporter himself meets his part of the contract; the lender will, therefore, still need to be convinced of the reliability of the exporter, and credit insurance is no guarantee against his failure. In the case of bank guarantees the general tendency is for banks to restrict lending to the portion of the transaction covered by the guarantee: in other cases the amount lent depends partly on the credit-worthiness of the exporter and partly on the length of the contract and the actual amounts involved.

The Radcliffe Report (see *Bib.* 72) commented:

"So far the finance of export credit, once guaranteed by the ECGD, does not appear to have presented any serious problem; there has been no apparent lack of finance for exports within the limits effectively imposed by the ECGD's 'five years from shipment' rule, and the finance provided has come almost entirely from the joint stock banks."

The position has not changed substantially in this respect in the decade since the Radcliffe Report; there have however been other developments. The Amstel Club for example is a group of leading financial houses in Western Europe and the United Kingdom, which have entered into reciprocal agreements for the financing of imports and exports between their countries. Credit is offered to the buyer for a period of up to two years on most classes of durable goods, whether for retail sale or sale to manufacturers (stocks may also be financed on shorter terms). The manufacturer is thus able to sell for cash and liquidate funds which may otherwise be tied up; and he has the additional advantage of not having to arrange the credit facilities himself.

Factoring too has increased in recent years in export markets; factors are always anxious to extend their range of profitable operation, and have in the past lowered their minimum turnover figures to assist potential exporters. Factoring can be particularly valuable in export markets, where money tied up in debtors can be immobilised for even longer periods than in domestic markets.

Many of the problems of export finance apply equally to large and small firms, but the small firm does have special problems, as in all other fields of finance. Even when ECGD cover is available, lenders may not feel prepared to take the risks associated with the possibility of failure on the part of the manufacturer to meet his part of the contract; and in addition even if 90 per cent. of the contract price is covered against default on the buyer's side, there may still be too big a risk of loss. The bigger these two risks are, the higher will be the cost of the finance. And the general problem of liquidity is even more serious with exports than with home sales: even short-term credit periods are longer (up to six months as compared with typical periods of up to three months on the home market); medium-term credit provides even more serious problems.

But correspondingly more effort has gone to the solution of these problems than to the financial problems arising from transactions on the home market, and the small exporter has facilities beyond those available to firms which do not export. At the best of times, however, exporting is potentially a hazardous business for the small firm, and the financial difficulties probably do little more than reflect this fact.

OTHER GOVERNMENT ASSISTANCE

Assistance for exporters grew up because Governments are concerned with the balance of payments; they are similarly concerned with regulating the level and direction of capital expenditure and with assistance to attract business to regions which suffer from particularly high unemployment.

Government inducements to capital expenditure normally come either through investment allowances against tax (which come under a variety of titles), depreciation allowances or through investment grants. The whole system is complex and is subject to periodic change.

The legislation current at the time of writing is the Industrial Development Act of 1966, which designated five broad areas as Development Areas; the areas are Northern England, Merseyside, nearly the whole of Scotland and Wales, and most of Cornwall and North Devon. Northern Ireland is not a Development Area but is covered by similar legislation.

Aid given is not exclusively financial; it includes advice on location, help in industrial training for workers, help under the nucleus labour force scheme (which provides assistance for unemployed local people transferred temporarily to parent works for preliminary training), and under the key workers scheme (which provides assistance for key workers transferred permanently or temporarily from the parent works to the Development Area); there may also be help in housing.

Financial aid comes in several forms. Investment grants on the capital cost of assets are available at the rate of 45 per cent. in

Development Areas, compared with 25 per cent. elsewhere. Buildings grants are at the rate of 35 per cent. in Development Areas and 25 per cent. elsewhere; loans may also be arranged at moderate rates of interest if projects create additional employment in Special Development Areas (districts in Development Areas affected by colliery closures). Buildings are available for rent or purchase, and exceptionally they may be rent free (in Special Development Areas this rent-free period may be as much as five years). Various other loans and grants may be available, and in manufacturing industry Regional Payments are also made, which may bring the employer as much in net benefit as 30s. per week per male employee. Most of these special benefits are confined to manufacturing industry; but hotels are eligible for other special forms of assistance, and service industries may be eligible if they bring substantial employment.

In Northern Ireland other assistance may come through industrial derating, fuel subsidy on the cost of fuel in manufacturing concerns, factories to rent at low rents ($7\frac{1}{2}$p to 14p per square foot) or even free for a period in some circumstances, grants towards special costs such as transfer of plant and machinery, grants towards operating costs in the initial stages of development, industrial advice grants towards the costs of consultancy, and Regional Payments. Following a recommendation in a recent report on the Northern Ireland economy (*Development Programme 1970–1975*), the Ministry of Commerce has established a Local Enterprise Development Unit, with the aim of tapping the potential for increased employment, particularly in smaller business undertakings in the outer areas; it will also provide a wide range of advisory services and engage in promotional and publicity activities for local enterprises.

Apart from the investment grants, few of these special inducements are given automatically, and whether or not a business will qualify for aid depends on the contribution which it makes to local employment. The government authorities have discretion in most cases; generally speaking they are keen to help. A series of Board of Trade booklets on development areas is available.

Whether or not the various financial and other inducements will be sufficient to persuade the owners of a new business to set up in or transfer to a Development Area or Northern Ireland depends very much on individual circumstances. If there are other reasons why businesses should not set up in such areas, the inducements may not be sufficient to counter-balance them. But the grants and allowances may well be of help to individual businesses, and the small firm may derive substantial benefits from setting up in these areas rather than elsewhere, provided that the area does not possess any specific disadvantages.

Although publicity usually goes to the bigger business which establishes a new plant in a Development Area or Northern Ireland, this should not obscure the fact that the assistance is available for small businesses as well. In Northern Ireland and some of the other areas it is recognised that a number of small concerns creating about a hundred new jobs each can make a big contribution to local problems; this contribution is all the more attractive in that it may bring with it more diversification, smaller reliance on a few industrial giants, and the fact that small owner-managed businesses tend to become identified with the local community is another point in their favour.

But it is up to the owner of the business to make the initial approaches and to be prepared to make a good part of the subsequent running.

THE FINANCE OF AGRICULTURE

Agriculture is par excellence an industry of small businesses.

A study in 1962 (see *Bib.* 75) described the financing of a group of seventy-two small farms in Cornwall, Devon and Dorset over the period 1949 to 1959. Of total incoming funds in that period of just over £1 million, 87 per cent. was gross farm income (or earnings), 4 per cent. was from gross receipts outside the farm, and only 9 per cent. was from increased borrowing. The spending of the money was accounted for by: 36 per cent. on family living; 51 per cent. on investment in land, buildings, machinery, livestock, crops, stores, etc.; financial assets increased by 8 per cent. The inclusion of family living complicates the picture, but leaving that out shows that between 55 and 60 per cent. of total funds raised came from retained profits: not vastly dissimilar from firms in the rest of the economy. A substantial part of borrowing came from family loans, and a great deal from increases in bank overdrafts (though several farms in fact reduced these). The number of farms with overdrafts rose from eighteen to thirty during the period, the average size of overdraft rose from £476 to £1,646; the commonest reason for incurring a new overdraft being the purchase of plant and equipment. During the period there was also some increase in the amounts owing to creditors. Trade creditors and debtors account for a relatively small proportion of balance-sheet liabilities and assets: creditors were only 7·3 per cent. of net assets, debtors were 3·7 per cent. in the period 1958–1959; bank overdrafts were 6·1 per cent., as also were long-term loans and mortgages.

The general picture is of a high degree of self-financing in small farms. The authors of the study ask whether this traditional method can be expected to provide sufficient funds in the future, when the trend towards owner-occupation, and away from the landlord–tenant system, may be expected to raise the capital needs of farmers. They doubt whether "... the process of capital accumulation can continue for the small business unit." This is not unlike the problem which faces many small firms in manufacturing industry and the distributive trades.

The Radcliffe Committee also investigated the problems of agricultural credit and examined the main sources. First came the joint-stock banks (the proportion of total bank advances going to agriculture averages 11 per cent., compared with agriculture's contribution of 4 per cent. to the gross national product), next came credit from agricultural merchants and livestock dealers, and hire-purchase. Various long-term sources also exist, such as the Agricultural Mortgage Corporation, the Lands Improvement Company, the Scottish Agricultural Securities Corporation, and the Agricultural Loans Fund (Northern Ireland); the Exchequer is also an important source of credit; and insurance companies are a source of mortgages.

Two main propositions were examined by the Radcliffe Committee: first was "... that the existing sources of credit do not adequately provide for the requirements of credit-worthy farmers"; second was "... that the rates of interest charged on loans to farmers tend to fluctuate too widely and rise too high." The conclusions of the Committee were: that there was no obvious gap in the credit facilities such as would justify a new institution; that banks should continue to be the main source of credit, but that there was room for improvement of the farmers' understanding of what the banks could offer; that banks should be prepared to offer term loan facilities "within reasonable limits"; they refused to support any proposals for a concessionary rate of interest for agricultural borrowers, and considered that any support given to agriculture should continue to be given through the general system of subsidies.

This is a cursory review of the financial problems of agriculture; but it is sufficient to bring out the fact that small farms, like all other small business units, depend heavily on their own savings for the provision of long-term capital, and rely a great deal on the banks, trade credit and hire-purchase for their other needs. The conditions under which agriculture operates are different from those facing manufacturing industry and the distributive trades—in particular farms work under a complex system of subsidies, price reviews and guarantees—but in essence the financial problems of small farms are similar to those of all small businesses.

The problems of small rural firms were also brought before the Radcliffe Committee in a memorandum by the Development Commission, which pointed out the difficulties experienced by such firms and singled out a series of special cases. These were: the need for permanent working capital for stock, wages, etc.; the need for funds for the taking over by a young person of an established business; the general expansion of an existing business; the establishment of a business of a traditional type in an area where it is needed; and the introduction of a new industry into a rural area. One of the main problems of small rural firms is that they do not need enough money. Specialised financial institutions do not normally consider loans of less than £5,000; but the small rural firm rarely needs more than a few hundred pounds. Since it is frequently in the nature of their problem that they do not have a good past record of profitability, they are unable to raise funds from banks without special guarantees; they also face the problem that suppliers are unwilling to give credit to small firms which may be relatively recently established and which place relatively small orders. There are possibilities for small rural firms in co-operation with each other to factor debts, insure debts, or buy supplies collectively (as farmers occasionally do); but since rural industries are usually collections of individuals, it is usually left to advisory bodies to organise and help such schemes on their way.

In general, government assistance and advice for small businesses is available on a fairly wide scale, ranging from the Council for Small Industries in Rural Areas, through NRDC, ECGD, the National Economic Development Office and the "little Neddies" for various industries, the Industrial Reorganisation Corporation (now to be wound up), which was charged with the task of facilitating mergers and the promotion of industrial efficiency, to the Ministry of Technology itself, which now carries responsibility over a wide range of economic, financial and general business activities.

In far too many small businesses the owners display an unrealistic and thoughtless contempt for government intervention and assistance; although in many cases their behaviour may appear to suggest the contrary, Government and other official bodies exist to serve the community and, to the extent that there are ways in which owners of small businesses may benefit, they are foolish not to do so.

CHAPTER 10

MERGERS AND TAKE-OVERS

At various stages in their business career, many owners of small businesses are faced with the prospect of a merger, or being taken over. A merger is normally defined as a marriage between equals, where two companies join to form a larger, stronger unit; there may or may not be an exchange of money. The take-over, on the other hand, consists of buying up another company in order to acquire some specific asset; it may take place with or without the consent of the party being taken over. Mergers between equals are very rare indeed, and most cases which claim to be such are normally marriages between a stronger and a weaker partner; it is only realistic to recognise this fact at an early stage, and to save a great deal of later heart searching and disappointment.

There are several reasons why one course or the other might be attractive.

The main interest of many people, in business as well as in other fields where it is more generally recognised, is in creation, and they are less interested in the running of going concerns. They are happy to build a garden, or a house, or to write a play, or to build up a business, or a department; when it comes to the weeding, the maintenance, the daily running and so on, they are less interested and look for fresh fields to conquer. If such a businessman has created something which someone else wants and is prepared to pay for, an offer on his part to be taken over is quite a reasonable commercial proposition. But it is perhaps the uncommonest reason of all for being taken over.

A much more common reason is the attempt to cure a financial embarrassment; to be taken over in these circumstances is only feasible if the company offers both long-run potential and some asset (such as a product, or a licence, or a market, or property, or management) for which the buyer is prepared to pay.

Financial embarrassment or not, there may also be opportunities for a businessman to leave his business because it represents a profitable opportunity to sell it as a going concern.

Another occasion arises when a businessman is approaching the end of his career and must face up to the fact that he must relinquish control. If he has a successor, inside or outside the family, he may not have to worry, but many businessmen do not have successors to hand; it is no doubt a sign of bad management that they do not, but it happens, and they may still have businesses which are worth selling.

Finally there is the unsolicited take-over by some other business which has spotted the smaller one as something with a potential which it is prepared to buy.

This raises the main point, that mergers or take-overs will take place only if there is a profitable opportunity for someone. In the straight merger there may be for example some advantages from the pooling of financial resources, or production capacity, or there may be some economies to be obtained in the development of a marketing strategy on a larger scale, or there may simply be some advantages in pooling managerial skills and ideas. The main problems arise over who is going to run the merged company; the best man to be boss will not necessarily be the one who brings most in the way of material resources, but it is not always easy to convince the other partners. In cases like this, both companies should be clear in their own minds what it is they have to offer, what they have to gain, and what is the realistic price to pay, in terms of what to give up to achieve their aims.

There are many more motives for take-overs, which may be carried out with or without the consent of the shareholders of the taken-over company (the closely held private company should not very often find itself in the position of being taken over without being aware of the fact). The bidder may be attempting to get control of some asset which he sees in the business, and which he feels he could exploit more effectively; this may be some invention, or it may be a piece of property which is not realistically valued in the balance sheet, or it can even happen that the taken-over company's liquid assets may exceed the purchase price (there are not so many examples of such cash gifts to take-over bidders as there were, but smaller concerns with an unbalanced passion for liquidity may present such an opportunity). It may be management which he is after, but that is not likely to be a common motive in most take-overs of small businesses. On the other hand, the reason may be simply to stop competition or to stop the smaller company from making a nuisance of itself. In many cases of this sort the owner or owner-manager of the small business may have to face up to the fact that he will be out of a job when the deal is complete, and it is up to him to make sure that he gets the best terms for himself.

He must also make sure that his staff is looked after as well as he can, and he must be prepared to tell them as much in advance as possible what is going to happen. And if he is not the only shareholder, he must try to make sure that the other shareholders get a fair deal. These things are easier to arrange if the owners are not taken by surprise, and if they have taken some initiative themselves they should be all the better prepared.

Take-overs and mergers have become such an important part of the business scene that government, the City and the business community have taken steps to try to ensure that some orderliness and fairness should rule in take-over and merger transactions. The City Code was drawn up to provide rules for take-over bidders; although it is largely a voluntary code, it is frequently observed, and when it is not there is usually some publicity about the fact. The Government also has the power to refer proposed mergers of big companies to what used to be the Monopolies Commission, but what is now part of the new Commission on Industry and Manpower; the Government's concern goes even further, and the erstwhile Industrial Reorganisation Corporation was created partly to facilitate mergers which may lead to increased business efficiency.

For the smaller business, which has to live in a world of take-overs and mergers, and which may want to take advantage of the situation, the simplest rule of all is to be prepared to be taken over, to be prepared to take the initiative, and to be prepared for what may happen afterwards to owners and employees (and even customers, who have been known to suffer when take-overs have occurred). It is normally better to be the active seeker for a take-over, if only because that means that the business will have made some plans. The business should also have made an objective and realistic assessment of what it can offer and what it can expect to gain from a merger; these would include marketing prospects, both in terms of economies of scale, distribution facilities, and new markets, new products, new sources of materials, financial resources, innovations and technological resources, management skills and general profit opportunities. Corporate plans are often gimmicky and full of complicated and unnecessary rigmaroles which are not wanted in the small business, but the planning approach does have the merit that it enables the business to identify and assess these opportunities.

The owners should also go a stage further and try to identify possible partners or bidders which can meet the requirements of the company; further, they should have a list of those who they do not wish to join in any way. To meet both circumstances reasoned cases for and against not merely help in preparation; they also impress the other party and may lead to a better deal on that count.

If the owners do not want to be taken over, after due consideration of the pro's and con's; they must be prepared to defend themselves not merely from bids but also from the arguments of those, inside and outside the business, who would persuade them otherwise.

The other members of the company, the staff, the management and the employees all have a legitimate interest in the future of the business, and are not likely to be very impressed by the owners who do not take them into their confidence as much as possible. Some secrecy is always likely to be necessary, but it is an unfortunate charactersitic of many owners of small business that they like to play every card as close to their chest as possible; it does not always pay to do so. Neither are staff likely to be much impressed by such empty phrases as "wider opportunities" and so on, which the boss may trot out in the attempt to get them on his side. Unpleasant things can happen after mergers, and it is dishonest to deny the fact, or to try to prevent those who are likely to be affected from doing something to protect themselves. This fundamental truth affects the owners as well, who must be prepared for the fact that life will never again be the same after a merger; the company will lose its identity, the boss may lose his supreme position, or he may have a supreme position in a totally different set up and will have to learn to cope with that situation.

The owners should know their price for a merger or take-over, and should stick to it. If the company is not closely controlled it may not be easy to fight off a merger or take-over simply through financial and voting control; in such cases objective assessments and the ability to argue the case convincingly are all the more important.

And finally, as in most financial matters, the small business will do better if it takes sound advice early on. Financial matters are hardly ever best left to amateurs, however shrewd and hard-headed they may think they are.

CHAPTER 11

FURTHER IMPLICATIONS*

THE financing pattern of the typical small business is as follows: it has fairly low profits, but retains a good proportion of them and relies heavily on its own savings as a source of funds; it makes little use of long-term capital; it depends fairly heavily on borrowing from the bank and occasionally on loans from directors; it both gives and receives large trade credit, which may be a vitally important source of funds; occasionally it employs hire purchase or leasing. The biggest part of its funds therefore comes from its own resources and from short- and medium-term borrowing.

The most striking single fact about small growing firms is that they use every possible source of funds as frequently as they are able and are hungry for all of the funds which they can secure.

Growing concerns are of particular interest. H. F. Lydall (see *Bib.* 54) found that most of the businessmen interviewed in the Oxford Survey wanted to grow: 51 per cent. wanted to increase in size by up to 100 per cent.; 21 per cent. wanted to double in size or more; only 28 per cent. wanted to stay the same size. Not surprisingly young men were more ambitious than old. The chief hindrances to growth mentioned were lack of demand and shortages of basic factors of production in the form of factory space, labour and finance.

There is probably a stage of take-off in the growth of a business. Up to a certain point it is likely that the firm depends heavily on its own resources and short-term funds, and may have difficulty in growing. After take-off it may have larger internal resources and may be able, by virtue of its better established position in general, to use long-term external funds and to grow largely from its own momentum. There may be one or more such stages in the growth of a business. This is not to argue that the rate of growth is determined entirely by financial considerations, and indeed there is plenty of evidence and argument to suggest that the ability of management to keep pace with growth is probably the fundamental determinant, but

---

* References to the Bibliography are indicated, *e.g.* see *Bib.* 25; the Bibliography is to be found on pages 177–181.

there are certain stages of growth where financial difficulties may predominate.

Although many of the problems of finance are common to all sizes of firm, the small business has its own peculiar difficulties in some fields.

Whether because of imperfect knowledge of opportunities, or because they are unable to offer the necessary security to lenders, or because of shortcomings in the market mechanism, there is no doubt that small private companies have less easy access to long-term capital than has the large public company.

The new financial institutions which have grown up in an attempt to fill the Macmillan Gap have made important contributions to the financing of a number of businesses, and the improvement may be expected to continue. The Radcliffe Committee (see *Bib.* 72) was much concerned with this problem and took evidence on the point; the general impression was that, with the limited funds available it had been necessary for the institutions to select the best propositions and to concentrate on providing funds to more credit-worthy concerns. More funds have been available in recent years, and these have made a marginal contribution to the problem.

Concentration on the most credit-worthy concerns is obviously sound policy from the point of view of the lender; it is sometimes argued, however, that if the activities of such institutions as ICFC are restricted to profitable businesses with demonstrably good prospects, it is difficult to see what these corporations do which could not be done by established institutions. This is not entirely fair to ICFC and similar bodies, which fill a gap in that they provide a substitute to the new issue market for firms which cannot use this channel, and they do provide financial backing for a number of firms which would find it difficult to obtain otherwise.

In a good many cases where a financial gap exists it does so because expansion would not be justified in the sense that prospective returns are inadequate. Many businesses are short of capital, but in a good many cases this is due as much to poor prospects as to a severe shortage of funds; they may not be credit-worthy by any standards. It is sometimes argued that the Macmillan Gap is a good thing precisely because its existence makes sure that a good many of the less efficient firms in the economy are squeezed out, or at least not encouraged to grow. There is little doubt that there are hundreds of small businesses which are inefficient, and their continued existence represents a misuse of resources in the economy; financial help to such firms would be largely wasted and would clearly come a long way down any national scale of priorities. But smallness itself is not a sign of inefficiency. Small businesses continue to exist for a variety of reasons, and in certain spheres play a valuable part in the working of the economy; it would be idle to pretend that such firms were never short of funds or, if they were, that their problems should be ignored. Similarly many firms are small because they are at an early stage of their growth; it is at such stages that it is difficult to demonstrate good prospective returns or to appeal to outside lenders.

Another line of argument is sometimes employed, which runs: the fact that most small firms finance a large part of their activities from their own savings is evidence that they are not short of funds and that they have overcome their financial problems. This deduction is invalid: there are many businesses which are self-financed because they have no alternative, and may be forced to depend excessively on short- and medium-term funds to finance their growth. To argue that the Macmillan Gap has ceased to exist because few unsatisfied borrowers can be found who are credit-worthy by traditional standards and because most firms are self-financed is simply to ignore the problem.

The Macmillan Gap is partly institutional in that, despite improvements, the range and scope of existing institutions are still small; it is partly economic in the sense that many small firms are not credit-worthy by any standards. There is an increasing tendency nowadays by newer institutions to employ more dynamic criteria of credit-worthiness; more progressive lenders are prepared to base their policy on prospects rather than on security as represented by assets and other forms of cover. Such criteria are more difficult and more costly to apply, since they require extensive investigation; it may be that one form of help for small businesses would be a grant to cover such investigations, which can turn out to be so expensive for the lender that they substantially reduce the margin of profit on lending.

It is worth recalling that on the subject of credit-worthiness the Radcliffe Committee (see *Bib.* 72; para. 935 of Report) said: "It is implicit in the situation of a rapidly growing small firm that it cannot offer altogether adequate security for the loan capital that it wants and cannot afford to borrow without some assurance that it will not be asked to make early repayment."

The Radcliffe Committee concluded that, on the whole, the existing institutions, with some modifications, were probably adequate, and that a better knowledge of them would help to fill the Gap. But there are probably still many firms which need funds for expansion, which may well be justified in the long run; it is not easy for them to get funds save at disproportionate risk.

As a consequence of the difficulties of raising adequate long-term funds, small businesses rely heavily on short- and medium-term sources of funds: this reliance is probably excessive, and in many cases too expensive. In a good many cases this excessive short-term borrowing is ill-founded; in a good many other cases it is simply inevitable and, provided that it is only temporary, not too serious a matter in the short run provided that the borrower is aware of what he is doing. But for the growing small firm there is no substitute for many of its needs, and some businesses pay too much to shareholders and directors and members of the family and put too little aside for development; if such a business then has to depend on short-term sources of funds its growth is ill-founded and could be better financed. Similarly many small firms run into the problems of over-trading because their financial management is bad and they have not made sensible arrangements. There are also businesses in which relatively high short-term borrowing is not excessive and merely reflects the nature of the business: in the clothing industry, for example, firms have relatively high bills for stocks and wages, which are sensibly met from short-term funds.

But there are still many small firms which, because they cannot raise long-term funds, are forced either to eschew growth or to borrow excessively on short term and at high cost in order to grow. These firms are faced by the Macmillan Gap, which they fill by short-term borrowing.

Part of the Macmillan Gap can be filled without the need for special provision; there are several ways in which finance could be channelled to small firms without too much need for special institutions to cater for their requirements.

The use of hire-purchase and plant leasing are two ways of financing growth, which are becoming increasingly important; they are not cheap, and they are not suitable for all cases, and they are not a last resort when all else has failed, but they are useful in appropriate circumstances.

The banks, too, fill an important part of the Gap. Here, however, there is a case for improvement in the form of the extension of a system of term loans. The big American banks who are now extending their British operations are prepared to provide funds on a term loan basis, and the movement may become broader based. If there is a case for a new institution in Britain it is probably for a body specialising in the provision of term loans on a sound commercial basis. The Canadian Industrial Development Bank might provide a model: it was set up in 1944 ". . . to make term loans to industrial enterprises which, because of their small size, or their lack of a sufficiently long earnings record, or complications in respect of the security they could offer, could not obtain term financing from other sources on reasonable terms and conditions" (Annual Report 1959). IDB has turned out to be a highly successful, professionally operated and profitable organisation.

The development of a market for the factoring of accounts receivable in Britain is another way in which the financial system could be improved from the point of view of small businesses: such a market is developing but, since factors cannot operate on a very small scale, it may be inappropriate for smaller businesses. One way in which small businesses could be helped is through a system of credit insurance for debts, which would help smaller businesses to raise funds on their guaranteed outstanding debts, and may also help in factoring. The Export Credits Guarantee Department might serve as a model. Anything which would help in improving the liquidity of small businesses would be valuable.

Another area in which some improvements might be possible is the extension of bill finance. The London Discount Market is a unique and highly sophisticated institution: its main function at present is dealing in government bills, but the discount houses could possibly come back in a bigger way into trade bills, particularly if the commercial banks were to take a bigger interest in this sort of business.

Collective self-help is a further possibility for small firms, although the cantankerous independence of many businessmen rules such things out for them. There are economies of scale in finance as in other forms of business activity, and it should not be impossible to devise schemes of co-operation by small businesses to factor and insure their debt, for example, and it may also be possible to obtain credit conditions or bulk buying rights from suppliers on a co-operative basis. Some small retailers and farmers work on a co-operative basis which is not vastly dissimilar, and within trade associations there is probably some scope for such action.

But even with these modifications, and with improved knowledge on the part of businessmen and their advisers, there is probably still a bit of a gap, and growth may still be inhibited in cases where it might be desirable. There are still many imperfections in the capital market which operate to the disadvantage of the smaller business, and there is still something of a shortage of risk capital for the smaller business.

The Small Business Administration in the United States is sometimes put up as a model for Britain. The SBA was described in some detail in the first edition of this book, and there is no point in repeating the description in detail. SBA was set up in 1953 and has three main functions: to render financial assistance to small firms, to obtain for them a fair share of government procurement, and to help in solving management and technical problems.

SBA has been widely criticised in the United States, and has had some difficulty in performing its first function effectively; it has, however, performed a very useful service in the dissemination of information about managerial, technical and marketing problems to small businesses. This last is perhaps the main feature of SBA which it would be worth examining more closely in the British case, where many of the problems of small businesses are simply problems of awareness of new developments in techniques, management and in the world about them. It would be much more difficult to put up a convincing case for a large-scale government-sponsored organisation in Britain.

The other feature of SBA which might be worth looking at closely is its system of ensuring a fair share of government contracts for small businesses; but the suggestion contains problems. Apart from the difficulty of defining "fair" (which might in the last analysis have to be a certain percentage), there is the problem of making sure that the Government gets value for its money from small business contracts and does not have to pay more for inefficient work. Perhaps the biggest problem of all, however, is that the Government is unpopular as a customer of small businesses: there is frequently far too much formality in its procedures and, much more serious when dealing with firms which have problems of liquidity, the Government is a very slow payer of its debts. It always does pay, but the business

may have to wait a very long time. Perhaps hand in hand with a fair
share of contracts should go a system whereby government debts
may be factored at a reduced rate by a special government department; this would not be a subsidy, because all that would happen
would be that the cost of slow debt collection would be passed to the
body responsible for it (the buyer). But such a body would have to
work quickly and with a minimum of red tape if it were not to add
yet one more to the burdens imposed by the bureaucratic processes
of government.

There is no case for a general subsidy for small businesses: society
cannot and should not be expected to find the resources. Investment
grants are available for small and big businesses: there is no doubt a
great deal of scope for improvement in their conception and administration, and there may be a case for slightly more generous grants
for small businesses if they are likely to generate increased efficiency,
but the case would not be particularly easy to sustain in the face
of competing needs for scarce resources. The Northern Ireland
Government has a scheme of advice grants for consultancy, and
these have been used to good effect by some smaller concerns as well
as by some bigger businesses; a pilot scheme was also tried in Britain
and the lessons of it may be used to construct an improved scheme.
One of the disappointing features of such schemes has been the low
response to them, particularly from smaller businesses; part of the
explanation may be that a certain level of managerial sophistication
is required before the owners of a business can identify the need for
consultancy and advice, and the schemes may not be getting at the
businesses which are most in need of their aid. If such schemes do
lead to improvements in managerial and operating efficiency,
however, they can be beneficial to all concerned, although there is the
additional problem that they can generate excessive subsidy con-
sciousness.

There are some areas in which such assistance could be particularly beneficial. Feasibility studies in marketing and financial
appraisal are things which many small businesses are not very skilled
at doing; similarly they are not particularly well equipped to do all of
the work needed for the appraisal and feasibility study of innovations. The move towards the establishment of small business centres
based on universities is a welcome one, and it could help to solve
many problems in this sphere.

It would also be extremely difficult to sustain a case for special tax concessions for small business, or for special dispensation from the provisions of the 1967 Companies Act. Tax is a burden to everyone; so is the provision of information and the filling in of forms, but it is not readily apparent that any of these burdens fall particularly on smaller businesses. If there were any special provision for small businesses it is in any case arguable that it should be restricted to those who are likely to improve their efficiency, and that would be a very difficult thing to determine. It is difficult in the field of tax reliefs to think up a scheme which does not turn out to be a subsidy in the last analysis.

It has also been suggested that one way in which smaller businesses could be helped is through the establishment of a long-term capital market for small business, and another refinement of this is that in return for the disclosure of financial and other information required under the 1967 Companies Act, private companies might be able to secure quotation for their shares on a special capital market. It is difficult to see how exactly such schemes would work. Markets of this sort require that investors should be prepared to buy on them, and one of the problems of the smaller concern is that it is frequently not able to offer sufficient attractions for investors to buy their shares, quoted or not. Take-over bids might be facilitated by such a market, but that may turn out to be a very mixed blessing. In all there would be a danger that such a capital market would be treated as a second division, and trading on it might come to be thought of as second-rate trade; the answer probably lies much more in the direction of the improvement of existing financial institutions, with special strategic help given in certain directions (as through term loans).

Perhaps the clue to the whole problem lies in the fact that the efficiently managed smaller business does not really find it so terribly difficult to get funds. It may be that they are inadequately informed of the possibilities, but part of efficient management consists of being aware of what is going on. It may also be that some lending institutions are too conservative and pay attention to asset cover at the expense of profit potential; in that case part of the answer lies in the institutions changing their ways. and this is already happening. But it would be too much to expect that every branch of every bank should have expert financial analysts capable of using the most up-to-date techniques and able to spare the time to carry out detailed analyses of small business proposals with all of their special difficulties.

Many of the financial problems of small businesses are due either to the fact that they are unsound commercial propositions or to the fact that their financial and operating management needs to be improved. A large part of business lending consists of backing the management, who must be able to demonstrate that they can use the money properly. Many small businesses fail in their applications because they have insufficient equity capital to satisfy the lender, or because there is too much loan capital from the proprietors, or because they cannot offer good unencumbered security, or because over-trading indicates bad financial planning; none of these on its own, however, would deter a potential lender if the borrower could put up a well-presented case backed by management potential. But small businesses are rarely very skilled at putting a good case or at presenting soundly conceived financial plans. This is partly because they are not skilled accountants, or they may lack good financial advice; this is an area in which some financial help by way of a grant for advice might make a contribution to the problem at low cost. Much more important, however, is that the lack of such skills itself may reflect inadequate management.

Businessmen are rarely their own best diagnosticians, and their reasons given for difficulty may not always be the right ones. An analysis of the failure of a hundred private companies was carried out by Dun and Bradstreet and published in the second issue of *Business Ratios*: the three most important reasons for failure given by the official receiver were, in order, mismanagement (in about 40 per cent. of cases), insufficient capital and insufficient working capital; the three main reasons assessed by the directors of the company were insufficient working capital, insufficient capital and bad debts (mismanagement was notably absent as a reason).

Management is partly a matter of sound technological skills, partly a matter of good management skills, not merely in finance but also in marketing, planning, control and communications, and in awareness of, if not necessarily an ability to, practise modern management methods; it is also a matter of providing good delegation and management succession. Not only are small businesses not very good at management, many of them are not very interested in improving it.

From the point of view of the small business, the lender and the economy as a whole, the long-term answer to the problem of small business lies in the improvement of management. It is a slow business, with few quick returns; it is also a perpetual problem as each new business which sets up will need to make good managerial deficiencies if it is to succeed. The smaller business is in a vicious circle: its management is rarely well-trained, and it is difficult for it to take time off to be trained; it can rarely afford, neither does it usually need, large-scale consultancy, and the larger consultants are not very interested in providing their services on a small scale. The strongest case for special treatment of small business is for advice, assistance and incentives in this field.

BIBLIOGRAPHY

THIS bibliography contains the titles of works referred to in the text, and a number of other references for further reading.
Numbers are to references in the text.

1. A. M. Alfred and J. B. Evans, *Discounted Cash Flow*, Chapman and Hall.
2. Association of Certified and Corporate Accountants, *Sources of Capital*, 1967.
3. H. S. Atherton, *Running the Smaller Firm*, British Institute of Management.
4. R. Banks (Ed.), *Managing the Smaller Company*, American Management Association, 1969.
5. James Bates, "Hire Purchase in Small Manufacturing Business," *The Bankers' Magazine*, September and October 1957.
6. James Bates, "The Finance of Small Business," *Bulletin of the Oxford Institute of Statistics*, May 1958.
7. James Bates, "The Finance of Small and Big Business," *The Bankers' Magazine*, April 1961.
8. James Bates, "The Macmillan Gap—Thirty Years After," *The Banker*, July 1961.
9. James Bates, "Financing the Small Business," *The Chartered Secretary*, March 1962.
10. James Bates, "The Macmillan Gap in Britain and Canada," *The Bankers' Magazine*, March 1962.
11. James Bates, "The Finance of Innovations," *The Bankers' Magazine*, July 1962.
12. James Bates, "The Profits of Small Manufacturing Firms," Chapter 10 in P. E. Hart, *Studies in Profit, Business Saving and Investment in the United Kingdom, 1920–1962*, Vol. I, Allen and Unwin, 1965.
13. James Bates, "Alternative Measures of the Size of Firms," Chapter 8 in P. E. Hart, *Studies in Profit, Business Saving and Investment in the United Kingdom, 1920–1962*, Vol. I, Allen and Unwin, 1965.
14. James Bates, "The Activities of Large and Small Companies," *Business Ratios*, Summer 1967.
15. James Bates, "Some problems in the interpretation of the accounts of unquoted companies," *Business Ratios*, Summer 1969.
16. James Bates and Michael Stewart, "Small Manufacturing Businesses: Accounting Information from a Pilot Survey," *Bulletin of the Oxford Institute of Statistics*, May 1956.

17. James Bates and S. J. Henderson, "Determinants of Corporate Saving in Small Private Companies in Britain," *Journal of the Royal Statistical Society, Series A*, part 2, 1967.

18. James Bates and S. J. Henderson, "The Determinants of Corporate Saving in Small Private Companies," Chapter 16 in P. E. Hart, *Studies in Profit, Business Saving and Investment in the United Kingdom 1920–1962*, Vol. II, Allen and Unwin, 1968.

19. James Bates and J. R. Parkinson, *Business Economics*, Second Edition, Blackwell, 1969.

20. Board of Inland Revenue, *Corporation Tax*, H.M.S.O., 1965.

21. J. F. Boswell, *ICFC Small Firm Survey*, Industrial and Commercial Finance Corporation Ltd., 1967.

22. Colin Bruce, F. A. Burchardt and E. B. Gibb, "Small Manufacturing Businesses: A Preliminary Report on a Pilot Survey," *Bulletin of the Oxford University Institute of Statistics*, August 1955.

23. *Business Ratios* (a Dun and Bradstreet/Moodies Publication); this journal ceased publication in the spring of 1970.

24. Board of Trade, *Companies General Annual Report* by the Board of Trade for the years ended December 31, 1949 to 1966 (annual publication).

25. *Companies, Annual Report*, H.M.S.O., 1968.

26. *Company Income and Finance*, National Institute of Economic and Social Research, 1956.

27. "Non-quoted companies and their finance," *Economic Trends*, February 1965.

28. R. S. Edwards and H. Townsend, *Business Enterprise*, Macmillan, 1959.

29. H. C. Edey, *Business Budgets and Accounts*, Hutchinson, 1959.

30. A. R. English, *Financial Problems of the Family Company*, Sweet and Maxwell, 1958.

31. Engineering Industries Association, *Financing Your Business*, 1967.

32. R. Evely and I. M. D. Little, *Concentration in British Industry*, Cambridge University Press, 1960.

33. *Financing Small Business*, Report to the Committee on Banking and Currency and the Select Committees on Small Business, United States Congress, by the Federal Reserve System, U.S. Government Printing Office, 1958.

34. G. R. Fisher, "Some Factors Influencing Share Prices," *Economic Journal*, March 1961.

35. P. S. Florence, *The Logic of British and American Industry*, Routledge, 1953.

36. P. S. Florence, *The Ownership, Control and Success of Large Companies*, Sweet and Maxwell, 1961.

37. R. A. Foulke, *Practical Financial Statement Analysis*, McGraw-Hill, 1953.
38. S. Friedland, *The Economies of Corporate Finance*, Prentice-Hall.
39. R. Frost, "The Macmillan Gap, 1931–1953," *Oxford Economic Papers*, June 1954.
40. S. Frowen, "Medium and Long-Term Finance for Small Businesses," *The Bankers' Magazine*, September 1960.
41. K. Grossfield, "Financing Innovations," *The Banker*, November 1961.
42. K. Grossfield, "Inventions as Business." *Economic Journal*, March 1962.
43. A. R. Hall, *Australian Company Finance*, Australian University, 1956.
44. P. E. Hart, "Business Concentration in the United Kingdom," *Journal of the Royal Statistical Society*, Vol. 123.
45. P. E. Hart and S. J. Prais, "The Analysis of Business Concentration," *Journal of the Royal Statistical Society*, Vol. 119.
46. R. F. Henderson, *The New Issue Market and the Finance of Industry*, Bowes and Bowes, 1951.
47. R. F. Henderson, "Comments on Company Finance," *Lloyds Bank Review*, January 1959.
48. T. G. Hutson and J. Butterworth, *Management of Trade Credit*, Gower Press, 1968.
49. H. Ingham and L. T. Harrington, *Interfirm Comparison for Management* (British Institute of Management). The Centre produces a number of other publications.
50. The Institute of Chartered Accountants in Scotland, *The Companies Act, 1967*, August 1967.
51. Institute of Cost and Works Accountants, *The Profitable Use of Capital in Industry*, Gee and Co., 1965.
52. F. R. Jervis, *Private Company Finance in the Post-war Period*, the Manchester School, May 1957.
53. H. F. Lydall, "The Impact of the Credit Squeeze on Small Medium Sized Manufacturing Firms," *Economic Journal*, September 1957.
54. H. F. Lydall, "Aspects of Competition in Manufacturing Industry," *Bulletin of the Oxford University Institute of Statistics*, November 1958.
55. H. F. Lydall, "The Growth of Manufacturing Firms," *Bulletin of the Oxford University Institute of Statistics*, May 1959.
56. A. Luboff, "The Finance of Public Companies," *Accounting Research*, October 1953.
57. A. Luboff, "Some Aspects of Post-war Company Finance," *Accounting Research*, April 1956.
58. Macmillan Report, *Report of the Committee on Finance and Industry*, 1931, Cmd. 3987.

59. E. C. McKean, *The Persistence of Small Business*, the W. E. Upjohn Institute for Community Research, 1958.
60. T. Mathews and C. Mayers, *Developing a Small Firm*, B.B.C., 1968.
61. A. J. Merrett and A. Sykes, *The Finance and Analysis of Capital Projects*, Longmans, 1963.
62. A. J. Merrett and J. Whitaker, "The Profitability of British and American Industry," *Lloyds Bank Review*, January 1967.
63. National Economic Development Council, *Investment Appraisal*, H.M.S.O., 1967.
64. National Science Foundation, *Science and Engineering in American Industry*, U.S. Government Printing Office, 1956.
65. F. W. Paish, *Business Finance*, Pitman.
66. E. T. Penrose, *Theory of the Growth of the Firm*, Blackwell, 1960.
67. Lord Piercy, "The Macmillan Gap and the Shortage of Risk Capital," *Journal of the Royal Statistical Society*, 1955.
68. Lord Piercy, "Financing the Small Business," *The Banker*, October 1961.
69. I. Pfeffer (Ed.), *The Financing of Small Business*, Collier-Macmillan, 1967.
70. S. J. Prais, "The Financial Experience of Giant Companies," *Economic Journal*, June 1957.
71. P. Quinn, "An analysis of the division of profits into taxation, dividends and savings in Northern Ireland public companies in the period 1961–1968 with special emphasis on the effects of the 1965 Finance Act," unpublished thesis for the degree of M.B.A., Queen's University of Belfast.
72. Radcliffe Report, *Report of the Committee on the Working of the Monetary System*, 1959, Cmnd. 827.
73. G. Ray and J. Smith, *Hardy Heating Co. Ltd.*, B.B.C., 1968.
74. D. Rea, "A Comparative Financial Analysis of Twenty-Six Indigenous Northern Ireland Public Companies," unpublished thesis for the degree of M.Sc.(Econ.), Queen's University of Belfast.
75. R. C. Richard, H. W. B. Luxton and S. T. Morris, "Financing the Farm Business," University of Exeter, Department of Economics, *Report No. 137*, November 1962.
76. R. T. Robinson, *Financing the Dynamic Small Firm*, Wadsworth, 1966.
77. T. G. Rose, *The Internal Finance of Industrial Undertakings*, Pitman, 1947.
78. E. Solomon, *The Management of Corporate Capital*, Collier-Macmillan Ltd., 1959.
79. J. Steindl, *Small and Big Business*, Blackwell, 1945.
80. *Survey of Current Business*, Washington, D.C., 1957.
81. Brian Tew, "ICFC Revisited," *Economica*, Vol. XXII, 1955.
82. Brian Tew, "Edith," *The Three Banks' Review*, June 1955.

83. B. Tew and R. F. Henderson, *Studies in Company Finance*, National Institute of Economic and Social Research and Cambridge University Press, 1959.
84. T.N.E.C. (Temporary National Economic Committee), Monograph 17, *Problems of Small Business*, Washington, United States Printing Office, 1961.
85. B. R. Williams and W. P. Scott, *Investment Proposals and Decisions*, Allen and Unwin, 1965.

Note: Both the Small Business Administration in the United States and the British Institute of Management in London publish on a regular basis a number of check lists and guidelines for small businesses. ICFC also publish valuable booklets and pamphlets on small business problems.

INDEX

Acceptance, 143
Acceptance credits, 143, 145
Accepting houses, 143, 144, 145, 147
Accepting Houses Committee, 143, 146
Accountants, advice of, 110
Accounting records, 36–45, 72
    problems in the interpretation of, 48–54
Accounting Research, 179
Accounts payable, 63, 122, 123
Accounts receivable, 26, 55, 122, 123, 171
"Accounts receivable" financing, 129
Acid test ratio, 47
Advertising, 11, 14, 25, 97
Age of firm, effects of, 125
Agricultural Loans Fund (Northern Ireland), 160
Agricultural merchants, 160
Agricultural Mortgage Corporation, 160
Agriculture and co-operative finance, 161
Agriculture, finance of, 159–162
Alfred, A. M., 177
Amalgamations, 94
American Research and Development Corporation, 150
Amount of finance required, estimation of, 28
Amstel Club, 156
Annual Abstract of Statistics, 3
Appropriation account, 83
Assets, 27, 36, 37, 39, 41, 52, 113, 116, 139, 159, 163
    revaluation of, 49
    valuation of, 48–50, 76, 78, 85
        See also Current assets, Fictitious assets, Intangible assets, Liquid assets, Net assets, Operating assets, Total assets
Association of Certified and Corporate Accountants, 177

Atherton, H. S., 177
Average rate of return method of evaluation of capital expenditure, 67–68

Bad debts, 40, 117
Balance sheet, 26, 35, 36, 37, 40, 41, 50, 93, 118
    tables, 18, 38
Bank advances, 113, 114
    in agriculture, 160
        See also Bank credit
Bank bills, 143
Bank borrowing, 21, 48
    individual firm, and the, 117–121
Bank credit, 29, 30, 86, 100, 105, 112–121, 167
    agriculture, in, 160
    banker and, the, 113–117
    difficulty of measurement, 118
        See also Bank advances, Bank loans, Bank overdrafts
Banker, The, viii, 177, 179, 180
Bankers' Magazine, The, viii, 177, 179
Banking profession, changes in, 117
Bank loans, 23, 45, 53, 64, 112–121, 139
    requirements of, 113
        See also Bank credit, Bank advances, Bank overdrafts
Bank managers, 110, 112–121
Bank of England, 103, 144
Bank of England Quarterly Bulletin, 114
Bank overdraft, 64, 100, 112, 113
    See also Bank advances, Bank credit, Bank loans
Bank rate, 115, 129, 146
Bankruptcy, 13
Banks, joint stock, 112–121, 143, 147, 153, 156, 160
    German, 112
    ICFC and, 104
    Macmillan Gap, and the, 170

Banks, R., 177
"Bar of size," 109
Bates, James, 48n., 177, 178
Bills of exchange, 126, 143–146, 153, 155
　costs of, 145
　defined, 143
　export trade, in, 144
　hire-purchase, and, 145
　principles of, 145
　problems for small firms, 146
Bills of Exchange Act, 1882, 143
"Block-discounting," 128
Board of Trade, 8, 152, 178
　booklets, 158
　President of, 16, 153
Bolton Committee, ix
Bolton, John, 16
Bonus issues, 37, 43, 53, 95, 96
Boswell, J. F., 21, 77, 99, 104, 105, 119, 123, 178
Break-even analysis, 35, 60–62, 72
Break-even charts, 43, 61
British Institute of Management, 48, 179, 181
British Market Research Bureau, vii
Bruce, Colin, vi, 178
Budgeted balance sheet, 57
Budgeted profit and loss account, 57
Budgets, Budgeting, 25, 28, 29, 32, 35, 45, 54–58, 72, 116, 121, 141
　defined, 54
Building society, 96
Bulletin of the Oxford University Institute of Statistics, 177, 178, 179
Bullion Market, 147
Burchardt, F. A., vi, vii, 178
Business Ratios, 48n., 175, 177, 178
Butterworth, J., 179

Cairncross, A. K., vii
Canadian Industrial Development Bank, 171
Capital
　cost of, 63–65, 68, 71
　forms of, 95–97

Capital—cont.
　form of—cont.
　　See also Long-term capital, Medium-term capital, Permanent capital, Short-term capital
Capital appreciation, 35, 107
Capital expenditure, 22, 75, 105, 142
　appraisal of, 62–72
　finance of, 29
　methods of evaluation of, 66–72
Capital expenditure budget, 57
Capital goods, finance of sale of, 30
Capital intensity, 51, 75
Capital issues, 92 et seq., 107
　See also New share issues, Share issues
Capital market, 22, 31, 104, 174
　imperfections in, 172
Capital structure ratios, 47
Capitalisation ratios, 99–100
Cash, 55, 86–87
Cash flows, 25, 34, 35, 37, 45, 54, 56, 66, 71, 72, 111, 117, 121, 142
Caution, self-financing, and, 89
Census of distribution, 5, 7
Census of production, 4, 73, 74
Central Office of Information, Social Survey Department, vi
Centre for Interfirm Comparisons, The, 48
Charges on assets, 101
Chartered secretary, the, 177
Charterhouse Group (also Charterhouse Industrial Development Co., and Charterhouse Organisation), 103, 147
City Code, The, 165
Close companies, 78–79, 81
Clydesdale and North of Scotland Bank, 116
Collective action, in finance and Macmillan gap, 171
Collective buying, in rural industries, 161
Commission, 145
Commission on Industry and Manpower, 165
Companies, importance of, 8–9

Companies Act, 1948, 49
  1956, 92
  1967, ix, 8, 16, 43, 49, 93, 94, 174
Competition, 10, 14, 24
  trade credit, and, 125
Concentration, 6
Concentration ratio, 6
Conditional aid scheme, vi
Confederation of British Industry, (CBI), 17
Confirming house, 153
Consultancy, 173, 176
Contracts
  long-term, finance of, 30
  short-term, finance of, 30
Control, 13, 14, 23, 24, 31, 33 et seq., 54, 98, 107, 164
Cost analysis, 59
Costing practices, 50
Costs, 73, 74
  bills of exchange, of, 145
Cost reduction, 59
Council for Small Industries in Rural Areas, 161
Credit, 140
Credit hunger, 126
Credit insurance, 127, 130, 153–157
  exports, for, 153–157
  Macmillan Gap, and the, 171
  rural industries, in, 161
Credit policy, 112
Credit-reporting agencies, 125
Credit Squeeze, The, 116
Creditors. See Trade Credit
Creditors' budget, 55, 57
Creditworthiness, 53, 106, 110, 115, 117, 125, 138, 143, 153, 156, 168
  Macmillan Gap, and the, 168–171
Current assets. 21, 40, 47, 52, 105, 115, 132
Current liabilities, 37, 47, 52, 100, 115, 136
Current ratio, 46–47

Death duties, 13, 92, 105, 147
Debentures, 22, 39, 97, 99, 101, 103, 147
Debt collectors, 125

Debt, long-term, 37, 39, 47, 53
  short-term, 23, 46
  See also Short-term funds
Debt versus equity problem, 31
Debtors. See Trade credit, Trade debtors .
Debtors' budget, 55, 57
Debts, collection of, 24, 123
Delegation, 14, 18, 175
Department of Social and Economic Research, University of Glasgow, vii
Depreciation, 22, 40, 41, 42, 49, 66, 69, 76, 79–81, 84–85, 141
Depreciation allowances, 157
Determinants of Corporate Saving in Small Private Companies in Britain, 52
Development areas, 97, 157–159
Development Commission, The, 161
Development Programme 1970–1975, 158
Differential rates, 118
Director-control, 21, 101
Directors' Loans, 20, 21, 23, 134–135, 167
  balance-sheet, and, 135
  bank managers, and, 135
  motives for, 134
Directors' Remuneration, 21, 23, 41, 51, 52, 79, 80, 84, 90, 135
Discount factor, 68, 69, 71
Discount houses, 127, 144, 171
Discount rate, 146
Discounts, 108, 128, 129, 131
Discounted cash flow, 68–71, 142
Discounting, 67, 71, 144
Disposable income, 81
Distribution of profits, policy towards, 81
Dividends, 21, 35, 39, 41, 51, 52, 64, 73, 78, 79–81, 86, 95
  directors' remuneration as alternative,
  importance of, 81
  policy towards, 94
Domination, by giant concerns, 14
Dun and Bradstreet, 48, 175
Durable plant, finance of, 30

Earning capacity, 75, 85, 96, 115
Earnings profile, the, 71
Ease of entry, 11
Economic Journal, The, 74, 178, 179, 180
Economic Trends, 18, 77, 83, 86, 178
Economica, 180
Economies of scale, 9–11, 13, 130
  finance, in, 171
  research, in, 148
Edey, H. C., 178
Edwards, R. S., 178
Efficiency, Macmillan Gap, and the, 168–169
  smallness, and, 169
"Eligible paper," 144
Employment, as size measure, 17
Endowment policies, 96
Engineering Industries Association, 178
English, A. R., 178
Enterprises and establishments in United Kingdom, 4
Equipment (and plant) leasing, 141–143
Equity, 23, 53, 64, 98, 134, 150
  capital, 77, 93, 117, 175
  interests, 107
  participation, 100, 103, 111
  See also Share capital
Equity Shares, 22
Establishment, defined, 1
Estate duties, 107
  See also Death duties
Estate Duties Investment Trust Ltd. (EDITH), 92, 107
Evans, J. B., 177
Evely, R., 6, 178
Exchange restrictions, 153
Exchequer, 160
Exempt private company status, 92
Expansion
  funds for, 23, 25–26, 29, 97
  possibilities for, 81
Export Credit Guarantees Department, 16, 153–156, 161, 171
  bank guarantees, 155
  comprehensive guarantees, 154
  policies, 154
  small exporter policies, 155

Export Credit Guarantees Department—*cont.*
  specific policies, 154
  terms, 155
Export markets, risks of, 152–157
Export trade, 129
Exports, finance of, 152–157
  risks of, 153–154
External capital, 92–111
  reasons for not raising, 109

Factories Acts, The, 16
Factoring, 128–130, 147, 156, 171, 173
  Macmillan Gap, and the, 171
  rural industries, in, 161
Family firms, 11, 13, 23, 101
Fictitious Assets, 115
Finance Act, 1965, ix, 81, 93
Finance Act, 1969, 81
Finance, as series of decisions, 28
Finance companies (houses), 25, 30, 63, 108, 127, 129, 131, 137, 138, 140, 142, 145
Finance Houses Association, 138, 140, 142
Finance
  principles of, 28–32
  Problem of, the, 14–17
Finance without recourse, 129
Financial institutions, 15, 67, 106, 129, 143, 146, 168, 174
Financial management, 170
Financial and operating ratios, 45–48
Financing of Small Business, 17
Fisher, G. R., 178
Fixed assets, 22, 39, 47, 49, 88, 122
  balance-sheet, in, 39
  valuation of, 49
Fixed charges, 115
Fixed costs, 60, 61
Fixed interest capital, 21, 64
Fixed interest payments, 31, 99, 104
Floating charges, 115
  debentures, 96
Flotation, 94
Florence, P. S., 178

Flow of funds statement, 43, 45
  analyses, 53
Forecasting, 36, 65, 72
Foreign exchange market, 147
Form of finance required, decision, 29–31
Forward planning, 28
Fothergill, J. E., vii
Foulke, R. A., 179
"Free issue materials," 128
Friedland, S., 179
Fringe benefits, 29
Frost, R., 179
Frowen, S., 179
Future tax reserves, 85–86

Gearing, 99–100
  ratios, 99
G.E.C. (General Electric Company), 47
Gibb, E. B., vi, 178
Goodwill, 129
Government assistance, 157–159, 162
  Northern Ireland, in, 158
Government restrictions, 139
Grants, 157, 158, 173, 175
Gross farm income, 159
Grossfield, K., 179
Gross profit, defined, 42, 76
Growing economy, effect on small firms, 12
Growth, costs of, 30–31
  effects of, 90
  finance of, 62, 90
  small firms, of, 167
  "take-off," and, 167
Guarantees, 115, 142, 151, 155–156
  agriculture, in, 161
  Export Credit Guarantee Department, of, 154–155

Hall, A. R., 179
Harrington, L. T., 179
Hart, P. E., vii, 177, 178, 179
Henderson, R. F., vii, 97, 113, 179, 181
Henderson, S. J., 178
Hire-purchase, 21, 23, 25, 29, 30, 32, 48, 119, 122, 127, 135–143, 145, 160, 167

Hire-purchase—cont.
  advantages of, 136
  charges, 137, 139
  conditions, 137
  criteria, 138
  deposits, 137
  disadvantages of, 139
  Macmillan Gap, and the, 170
  plank and equipment, of, 136
  repayment periods, 137
Historical cost, 40, 49
Hutson, T. G., 179
Hypothecation of Stocks, 115

Imperfections in capital market, 172
Income,
  appropriation of, 78
  distribution of, 80
  proprietors of small firms in the U.S.A., of, 13
Income statement, 40, 41, 43, 45
Income tax, 63
  See also Tax
Independence, 10, 11, 13
  fear of loss of, 106
Industrial and Commercial Finance Corporation (ICFC), 21, 22, 53, 64, 77, 100, 103–107, 113, 117, 119, 123, 151, 168, 178
Industrial Development Act, 1966, 157
Industrial Guarantees Corporation, 151
Industrial Holdings, 107
Industrial Re-organisation Corporation, 16, 161, 165
Industrial Training Act, 1964, 16
Industries and Trades, particular (and effect on financial behaviour), 1, 5, 6, 8, 9, 10, 75, 105, 108, 113, 114, 124, 127, 128, 130, 131, 136, 140, 146, 148, 158, 170
Ingham, H., 179
Inland Bills of Exchange, 126, 127
Inland Revenue authorities, 39, 49, 51, 79, 80, 84, 85, 178
Innovations
  Britain since Second World War, in, 152
  finance for, 147–152

Innovations—*cont.*
    part played by small firms, 148
    rewards from, 148
    risks of, 148, 149
Institute of Chartered Accountants in
    Scotland, 179
Institute of Cost and Works
    Accountants, 179
Institutional investors, 98, 103, 107,
    109, 150
    effect on capital markets, 22
Insurance companies, 25, 81, 96, 97,
    98, 107, 108, 110, 160
Intangible assets, 115
Interest (rates), 67, 84, 103, 115, 117,
    118, 132, 139, 160
Internal financial control, 29, 58–60, 72
Internal rate of return, 68, 71
Internal sources of funds, 23, 29, 103,
    140
Interstices, 12
Inventory control, 50
Investment, 88, 99, 100, 107, 108, 134,
    144
    agriculture, in, 159
    decisions, 62, 66
Investment allowances, 157
Investment appraisal, 63, 64, 66, 71
Investment companies, 96, 107
Investment grants, 16, 69, 157, 158,
    173
Investment trusts, 107, 108, 147
Issued capital, 22, 37, 39, 96
Issues (of shares)
    prospectus, by, 95
    shareholders, to, 95
    See also New Issue Market, Long-
        term capital
Issuing houses, 94, 95, 108
Issuing houses Association, 102, 147

Jervis, F. R., 179
Journal of the Royal Statistical Society,
    178, 179, 180

Kenning Organisation, the, 12
Key workers, 157
Knowles, K. G. J. C., vii

Labour management ratios, 47
Lagged dividends, 82
Lands Improvement Company, 160
Lease-back facilities, 108
Lease-or-buy decision, 97, 142
Leasing, 25, 167
    equipment, of, 141–143
    advantages of, 141
        See also Equipment leasing
Legal form,
    change of, 92
    effect on finance, 30, 31
Lending institutions, 15, 91, 106, 174
Letter of credit, 144, 145
Leverage, 99
Liabilities, 36, 37, 39, 41, 53, 113
Limited liability, 93
Linear programming, 71
Liquid assets, 47, 52, 60, 164
    as a source of funds, 86–87
Liquidity, 22, 32, 46, 47, 48, 53, 60,
    113, 164
    exports, and, 157
    measurement of, 86
Liquidity ratios, 46–47
Little, I. M. D., 6, 178
Livestock dealers, 160
Lloyds Bank Review, 179, 180
Loan capital, 30, 31, 48, 95, 101
Loans, 53, 84
    secured, 93, 103
    unsecured, 53, 96, 103
        See also Bank credit
Local Enterprise Development Unit, 158
London Discount Market, 171
Long-range plan, 33, 65
Long-term capital (long-term funds), 19,
    21, 22, 23, 25, 29, 30, 31, 89, 92–
    111, 112, 115, 116, 121, 160,
    161, 167, 168, 170
    forms of, 95–97
    problems of, 97–102
Long-term liabilities, 96–97
Low concentration group of British
    industry, 6
Luboff, A., 179
Luxton, H. W. B., 180
Lydall, H. F., vi, 167, 179

McKean, E. C., 180
Macmillan Committee (and Macmillan Report) (Committee on Finance and Industry, 1931, Cmnd. 3987), 15, 102, 107, 179
Macmillan Gap, 15, 105, 110, 120, 168–171
Macro-economics, 73
Maintenance costs, 141
Maintenance of capital value, 85
Maintenance of existing business, finance of, 29
Management and potential of a company, 54
Management by objectives, 65
Management problems of small firms, 13–14
Manufacturing establishments, size of, 2–3
Marginal costing, 61–62
Marginal propensity to save, 82, 83
Market imperfections, favouring small firms, 11
Market possibilities, 90, 151
Marketable Securities, 22, 40, 86
Marketability, 110
 of bills, 143
 of shares, 98
Marketing expenses budget, 57
Master budget, 57
Materials, 123
Mathews, T., 180
Maturity, of bills of exchange, 144, 145
Mayers, C., 180
Median, 73
Medium-term funds (medium-term credit, etc.), 23, 29, 30, 52, 90, 103, 113, 122–133, 134–143, 167
 reliance on, 170
Merchant banks, 25, 94, 107, 108, 110, 143, 146, 147, 153
Mergers, 163–166
 advantages of, 164
 defined, 163
 gains from, 165
 problems of, 164
 reasons for, 163–164
Merrett, A. J., 180

Midland Bank, 116
Ministry of Commerce for Northern Ireland, 158
Ministry of Technology, 161
Minority Shareholders (minority interests), 77, 84, 103
Montchiloff, N., vii
Monetary policy, 132
Monopolies Commission, The, 165
Morris, S. T., 180
Mortgage Debentures, 64, 96
Mortgages, 22, 37, 96, 97, 108, 115, 160
 in agriculture, 160
Motivation, 12

National Economic Development Office (Council), 161, 180
National Institute of Economic and Social Research, vii, 178, 181
National Research Development Corporation, 16, 148, 149, 150, 151, 161
National Science Foundation, 180
Nearly competitive type of British industry, 6
Net assets, 18, 39, 76, 82, 119
 defined, 76
Net output, 41, 74, 75
 ratios, 47
Net present value, 68, 71
Net profit, 42–43, 82
 defined, 76
Net worth, 39, 43, 47, 96
Nevin, E. T., 74
New issue market, 22, 79, 94–95, 102–110, 168
New share issues, 95 et seq., 101
 costs of, 97
  See also Capital issues, Share issues
Non-cash issues, 95, 96
Non-recourse finance, 129
Nucleus labour force scheme, 157
Nuffield Organisation, the, 12

Objectives, specification of, 33–34
Obsolescence, 141

Offer for sale, 95
Operating assets, 43, 88, 122
Opportunity cost, 64, 65, 71
Ordinary shares, 95, 107
Overdrafts, 21, 56, 112–121, 140, 147, 159
  advantages and disadvantages of, 117
  review of, 116
  variability of, 118
  See also Bank credit
Over-estimation of requirements, 28
Over-trading, 24, 25, 34, 52, 53, 126, 127, 132, 170, 175
Owners' participation, 91, 115
Ownership, 13, 14, 23, 98–99
  effect on finance, 31
Oxford Economic Papers, 179
Oxford Survey, the, 17, 18, 19, 20, 21, 22, 23, 37, 73, 74, 76, 78, 79, 80, 81, 83, 86, 87, 102, 108, 109, 118, 119, 123, 124, 134, 136, 139, 152, 167
Oxford University Institute of Statistics, v, vii

Paish, F. W., 180
Parkinson, J. R., 178
Partners, contribution of, 31
Partners' loans, 134
Payback method of evaluation of capital expenditure, 66–67
Penrose, E. T., 12, 180
Pension funds, 98, 147
Permanent capital, 30
Personal capital, 89
Pfeffer, I., 180
Piercy, Lord, 104, 108, 109, 180
Placings, 95, 98
Plant and equipment, purchase of, 159
Ploughed back profits, 20, 21, 87
Post-tax profits, 21
Prais, S. J., 81, 87, 179, 180
Preference shares, 77, 95, 99, 101, 107
Price/earnings ratio, 64
Price reviews, 161
Principles underlying financial decision, 28

Private companies
  formation of, 92–93
  registration of, 93, 94
Private company status, advantages of, 92–93
Private individuals, loans from, 135
Private investment funds, 147
Production budget, 57
Production planning, 12
Production time-lags, finance of, 30
Profit(s), 21, 52, 73, 79, 90
  distribution of, 23, 78–81
  effects on gearing, 99
  functions of, 73
  retention of, 23, 33
  turnover, on, 76
  valuation of, 51–52
  See also Retained profit
Profit/capital employed ratio, 46, 48, 75
Profit and loss account, 85, 93, 115
Profit/net asset ratio, 76, 77
Profit planning, 35–36, 72
Profit records, 106, 113
  in rural industries, 161
Profit/sales ratio, 46, 48, 75
Profitability, 13, 21, 73–78, 90, 113, 115, 116, 117, 119
  measurement of, 75–78
Promissory notes, 155
Proprietors, 13
Prospective returns, 168
Prospects, 117, 168
  demonstration of, 101
Public companies, 93–94

Quinn, P., x, 180

Radcliffe Committee (Radcliffe Report), (Committee on the Working of the Monetary System, 1959, Cmnd. 827), ix, 1, 15, 101, 102, 104, 108, 110, 116, 124, 127, 131, 132, 144, 147, 149, 150, 151, 156, 160, 161, 168, 169, 170, 180
Radcliffe Gap, 151
Ray, G., 180
Rea, D., x, 180

Regional payments, 158
Registrar of companies, 93
Renting, 97
    of plant, 141
    of premises, 25
Repayment of Bank Loans, 115
    See also Bank credit
Replacement cost, 49
Replacement theory, 71
Resale price maintenance, 11
Research, 148
Research organisations, 149–151
Reserves, 37, 39, 41, 81
    capitalisation of, 37, 94, 95
Retail establishments, size of, 5
Retail trade, 5, 6
Retained earnings, 39, 65
Retained profit, 19, 22, 24, 31, 43, 63,
    73, 78, 79, 81, 87, 122
    defined, 85
Revaluation of assets, 43, 49
Richard, R. C., 180
Rights issue, 95
Risk capital, shortage of, 172
Risks, of small firms, 13–14
Robertson, D. J., vii
Robinson, R. T., 180
Rose, H. B., 124, 127, 131
Rose, T. G., 180
Rural industries, finance for, 161

Safety requirements, 29
Salaries, 51, 80
    See also Directors' remuneration
Sales, 118
    See also Turnover
Sales budget, 57
Sales/capital employed ratio, 46, 48
Saving(s), 21, 22, 29, 73, 79, 84, 89–91
    agriculture, in, 161
Savings/expenditure ratio, 88–89
Savings/investment ratio, 88
Schedule F Income Tax, 93
Scott, W. P., 181
Scottish Agricultural Securities Cor-
    poration, 160
Secondary Credit and Performance
    Ratios, 47

Security, 101, 113, 116, 127, 137, 142,
    145, 146
Self-financing, 22, 87–89, 169
    agriculture, in, 160
    financial needs, and, 90
Self-liquidating debt, 30
Semi-durable plant, finance of, 30
Services for British Exporters, 152
Share capital, 8, 22, 30, 31, 37, 39, 43,
    48, 64, 94, 95, 96, 103, 147
Share issues, 19, 22
    See also Capital issues, New share
    issues, Issues
Shareholders, 35, 39, 81, 95, 97, 101,
    164, 165, 170
"Shortfall assessment," 79
Short-term capital, 19
Short-term funds (short-term credit),
    23, 29, 30, 52, 60, 90, 100, 103,
    112–121,   122–133,   134–143,
    144, 153, 167
    reliance on, 170
Short-term liabilities, 40, 86, 87, 132
"Sight bill," 144
Size,
    effects of, 22, 23
    efficiency, and, 169
    measures of, 17
Small business,
    defined, 14, 16, 17–18
    importance of, 1–17
    persistence of, the, 9–12
    problems of, 13–14
Small business administration, 172
Small Business Survey, v, vi, vii, ix
Small-scale industry, factors favouring,
    9–12
Smith, J., 180
Solicitors, 110
Solomon, E., 180
Solvency, 36
Sources and uses of funds, 19, 43, 44
    statements of, 36, 37
Sources of funds, 20–21, 25–26
    outside, reasons for not trying, 109
    See also Internal funds, Long-term
    funds,   Medium-term   funds,
    Short-term funds

Special development areas, 158
Specialist institutions, 26, 102–109
Stamp duty, 145
Steindl, J., 10, 11, 180
Stewart, M. J., vi, 177
Stocks, 21, 22, 33, 40, 45, 47, 48, 59, 75, 88
  hypothecation of, 115
  peaks, finance of, 118
  valuation of, 50
Stock control, 59
Stock exchange, 89, 95
Stock exchange introduction, 95
Stock exchange securities, 63, 145
  See also Marketable securities
Stockbrokers, 108
Studies in Company Finance, 119, 181
Subsidiary companies, investments in, 115
Subsidies, in agriculture, 160
Superannuation funds, 147
Suppliers, 108
  connection with, 108
Sykes, A., 180
Synergy, 9

Tabulating Research Centre, London, vii
Take-off, 167
Take-over bid, 14, 81, 174
Take-overs, 163–166
  defined, 163
  reasons for, 163–164
Tax (Taxation), 16, 21, 41, 49, 52, 69, 79, 84, 85, 86, 101, 118, 141, 174
  burden of private companies, 79
  effect on self-financing, 79
Tax legislation, 78
Tax refunds, 54
Tax Rescue Certificates, 40, 86
Technical Development Capital Ltd., 150, 151
Temporary National Economic Committee, 181
Term Bill, 143, 144
Term Loans, 116–117, 160, 174
  Macmillan Gap, and, 171
Tew, Brian, vii, 88, 180, 181

Three Banks Review, The, 180
Time value of money, the, 67–68, 71
Times, The, 47
Timing, of raising of funds, 29
Tooling charges, 128
Total assets, 22, 47
Townsend, H., 178
Trade Bills, 143
Trade credit, 21, 23, 43, 45, 48, 87, 119, 122–133, 167
  agriculture, in, 161
  as form of competition, 125
  banks, and, 127
  composition of, 122
  costs of, 130–133
  dangers of, 132
  difficulty of measuring, 123
  financial factors affecting, 125
  financial weakness, and, 130
  financing of, 126–128
  importance of, 122
  net, defined, 123
  policy towards, 125
  retailers, and, 127
  rural industries, in, 161
  seasonality of, 123
  small and big business, in, 122–126
  stocks, and, 123
  terms of, 131
  turnover, and, 123
Trade creditor/debtor ratio, 124
Trade creditors, 30, 45, 52, 115, 119, 122
  agriculture, in, 160
  overvaluation of, 124
  payment of, 32
Trade debtors, 52, 112, 115, 122
  agriculture, in, 160
  operating asset, as, 122
  undervaluation of, 124
Trade investments, 40, 96
Trading account, 42, 45
Trading and profit loss account, 41, 42, 43
Trading profit, 79
  See also Profits
Transferability of shares, 98, 107
Trend indices, 47

Turnover, 17, 51, 56
 debtors, and, 125
Turnover/net asset ratio, 76

Underestimation of requirements, 28
Undervaluation of assets, 76, 87
Undisclosed factoring, 129
Undistributed income, 85
 See also Profits, Retained profits
Unemployment, effect on small firms, 12
Unincorporated business, vi, 8, 92
Unit trusts, 98, 147
United States economic aid, vi

Valuation of assets, 49–50
 fixed assets, of, 49
 stocks, of, 50
Valuations, and bank credit, 115
Value added, 41, 43, 47, 73, 74, 76
Value added ratios, 47

Value analysis, 59
Variable costs, 60, 61
Vertical integration, 50
Vice, Anthony, 47
Voting control, 106, 166
Voting power, 81
Voting rights, 31

Wear and tear allowances, 84, 141
Weinstock, Arnold, 47
Welfare provisions, 29
Whitaker, J., 180
Wholesale establishments, size of, 7
Wholesale trade, 6, 7
Williams, B. R., 181
Windfalls, 89
Window dressing, 119, 135
Work in progress, 21, 48, 105
Working capital, 16, 60, 69, 87, 88, 105, 112, 118, 141
 for rural industries, 161